Education for Citizenship: Ideas into Action

Education for Citizenship: Ideas into Action is a practical, accessible handbook for teachers wishing to incorporate this new area into the curriculum. The book covers the full range of themes identified within the framework for citizenship education in the National Curriculum. It not only provides teachers with useful material which can be immediately incorporated into their classroom practice, it also gives a practical grounding in citizenship education with useful summaries of the latest research.

Key themes are:

*   social and moral education

*   community understanding and involvement

*   language skills and media literacy

*   democratic processes and political literacy

*   cultural diversity and global citizenship

*   human rights and environmental issues

The book includes case studies, examples of pupils' work, suggested teaching strategies and innovative photocopiable materials which have been successfully trialled in schools. There is also a comprehensive reference and resources section. It is an invaluable resource for teachers of the 7–14 age range, curriculum co-ordinators and those wishing to know more about the thinking behind education for citizenship.

Nick Clough is Principal Lecturer in the Faculty of Education, University of West England, Bristol.
Cathie Holden is Senior Lecturer in the School of Education, University of Exeter.
Harriet Seddon completed the illustrations whilst in her final year at school. She is now studying Art & Design.

Education for Citizenship:
Ideas into Action

A Practical Guide for Teachers of Pupils aged 7–14

Nick Clough and Cathie Holden

Illustrated by Harriet Seddon

London and New York

First published 2002
by RoutledgeFalmer
11 New Fetter Lane, London EC4P 4EE

Simultaneously published in the USA and Canada
by RoutledgeFalmer
29 West 35th Street, New York, NY 10001

RoutledgeFalmer is an imprint of the Taylor & Francis Group

© 2002 Nick Clough and Cathie Holden for text and Harriet Seddon for illustrations

Typeset in Gill Sans by Exe Valley Dataset Ltd
Printed and bound in Great Britain by TJ International Ltd, Padstow, Cornwall

British Library Cataloguing in Publication Data
A catalogue record for this book is available from the British Library

Library of Congress Cataloging in Publication Data

Clough, Nick
    Education for citizenship : ideas into action : a practical guide for teachers of pupils aged 7–14 / Nick Clough
    and Cathie Holden.
        p. cm.
    Includes bibliographical references and index.
    1. Citizenship—Study and teaching (Elementary)–Great Britain. 2. Active learning—Great Britain.
    I. Holden, Cathie. II. Title.

LC1091 C529 2002
372.83'2—dc21   2001045711

ISBN 0-415-23431–X

Contents

Acknowledgements

The authors would like to thank all students and teachers who trialled the activities and all colleagues who read final drafts, in particular Professor David Hicks. We would like to dedicate this book to the young people in our lives, including Ben, Leo, Emily, James, Harriet, Theo, Alex and Anna Marette.

An Introduction to Citizenship Education

It's a breath of fresh air for schools (Secondary school teacher)

It's the core of quality education (Year 4 student-teacher)

It is radical and even subversive. In effect, it is nothing less than a blueprint for turning this nation of ours from a land of passive subjects into one of active citizens. (Ascherson N. 1998)

Nearly 2,500 years ago an audience of democratic Greek citizens gathered to see what would happen in Sophocles' play *Antigone*. This play presents a problem as challenging as any we find today. Antigone's brother has been killed and has been declared an outlaw of the state because of his political activity. Antigone has been forbidden by law to bury him. But without burial his soul will not be able to cross into the afterworld. What should Antigone do? Should she act as a sister and break the law to honour her brother and give him a decent burial? Or should she act as a good citizen and leave her brother's body to be eaten by scavengers?

You want to know what happens of course.

- Antigone did break the law to ensure that she behaved like a sister ought to.

- She won the approval of many as a virtuous person with moral substance.

- She became a refugee and was protected by kind shepherds.

- Two heroes, Heracles and Theseus, were called in to try to sort the matter out.

This story still features as content for the National Curriculum in England (history, Key Stage 2) and is a story for people in any time and any place. The ancient myth speaks to us through time about difficulties we often face in matters of values.

- How do I know what being good means?

- How do communities become fragmented?

- Where do I belong? To whom should I be loyal?

- What are my rights? What are my responsibilities?

- Should political views be outlawed?

- When should I take political action to change things?

- What is the right way to take action?

It is a story about freedoms, about rights and about conflicting obligations. It is more than a story about the individual and the state. It is about the relationship between self and collective, between self and all the institutions to which we are attached including family, communities and place of work.

Today's children also face dilemmas of split loyalties. They are learning to be citizens across the continuum of sometimes contrasting environments – the home, the street and the school. In many communities this can be a complex experience as described by a parent in a recent interview for a study into citizenship education.

> *The issue is the children's identity within the environment. The difficulty of marrying their cultural identity with what they see everyday at school or everyday when they are out with their friends. There are things that they think are attractive, that are easy, ways of talking that are happening on the street. They want to be a part of that but in the home environment they know that is not what we are going to accept. I think there is a lot of dilemmas going on. There is a lot going on which is not necessarily understood or catered for. (Clough 1999)*

Where there are dilemmas there is a need for guidance, support and a set of values which can be upheld. This process is summarised by the philosopher Blackburn in his recent book 'Being Good'.

> We need standards of behaviour in our own eyes and we need recognition in the eyes of others. (Blackburn 2001: 133)

Such exploration of values occurs on a daily basis in schools across many countries in the world. What unites such diverse education programmes is that the values selected are themselves protected, mediated and given meaning through guardianship and agency of the United Nations (Starkey 1992). They are enshrined in the Universal Declaration of Human Rights:

> All human beings are born free and equal in dignity and rights. They are endowed with reason and conscience and should act towards one another in a spirit of brotherhood. (Article One)

This part of the curriculum is referred to as education for citizenship. A summary of the learning objectives that are included in the new National Curriculum in England (DfEE/QCA 1999) is presented in Handouts 6 and 7 for use during staff discussions. These outcomes endorse the political values of pluralism and democracy. The same National Curriculum document identifies that teachers should reaffirm commitment to a key set of virtues – **truth, honesty, justice, trust and a sense of duty** (DfEE/QCA 1999:10). The integration of these social values with the learning outcomes significantly enhances the focus of the programme, as is illustrated below. Of course schools may add their own values (for example inclusion, sustainability), according to the context of the school and the local community.

2

Examples of learning outcomes for citizenship education related to:

I   Truth

Teachers and learners will be concerned to:

- research topical and political issues, through collecting evidence from a full range of sources of information including those reflecting different perspectives

- understand self in relation to other

2   Honesty

Teachers and learners will be concerned to:

- explore how the media present information

- recognise stereotypes and other forms of unfair representation

3   Justice

Teachers and learners will be concerned to:

- understand that resources can be allocated in different ways and that these economic choices affect individuals and communities

- reflect critically on their own views of the lives of people living in other places and times and people with different values and customs

4   Trust

Teachers and learners will be concerned to:

- recognise that the voices of children should be heard

- recognise that the law of the land and Human Rights Conventions protect citizens

- understand how groups can work together to solve problems locally and globally

5   Sense of duty

Teachers and learners will be concerned to:

- ensure that children can and do participate in the decision-making process of the school

- challenge stereotypes and other forms of injustice.

Case study to exemplify the application of political and social values in a curriculum activity

This account refers to ongoing work with children in a primary school in Bristol about life in a rural community in Zimbabwe in Southern Africa. This is a pertinent piece of work because it takes place at a time when diplomatic relationships are fragile and news reports quite negative. In spite of this, contacts between the school and the village are being maintained to extend the horizons of community experience for these children. Links have been established and supported through the Zambuko (meaning 'bridge') Community Library Project and the Britain Zimbabwe Society. Musicians who had visited the village supported the project though teaching the children some dances and songs from the Bindura district where the village is located. One of the musicians, an mbira player, was himself brought up in this village. It is thus a curriculum project which accesses voices from the South.

The Bristol children noticed from evidence in photographs that the children in the village only have books in English. They learned that one of the aims of the Zambuko Library Project is to purchase a bookbinder so that new and relevant materials can be made to enable the children to learn to read in their own language, Shona.

Here are some questions asked by the English children after studying the photographs.

I would like to ask the builders some questions about what they think about the project. Do they like working as builders on this kind of project? What do you think the oldest man in the village thinks about it? Do you think he can remember other projects like this in the past?

I think it would be nice if when the library is built the children could get a cold drink when they first arrive to look at the books.

There was concern for **truth** here as the children identified questions that they wanted to ask the people in the photographs. The teacher was well placed to support this because the children had begun a conversation (so to speak) and were thinking beyond themselves and their own experience.

The children began to consider questions of **justice**. They discovered that the old man knew much about building because when he was 45 years old the village had been forcibly moved to its current location to make space for the development of a white Rhodesian farm. There were many subsequent questions about **honesty** as the children explored the many representations of the Shona people through different media, in the past through the colonial times and the war of independence and also in current reports on tensions in the country. There were conflicting accounts here which they had to appraise. As they found out more about the process of decolonisation, the vestiges of former trading patterns became apparent – for example, the controversial tobacco trade on which this village in part depends economically. Learning about **trust** emerged from this enquiry. They learned about arrangements that are in place to support this community and about how their support networks operate. They learned that the village is itself seen as a centre for spiritual healing and that many who are troubled depend on the skilful interventions of Dominic Mutambapadziri, a healer who lives there and is the leader of the community. For example one man visited because he had killed another man when he was a soldier in the war in the Congo. They also found out that the elderly are always accompanied and supported by younger community members. They learned about a **sense of duty** too and how those in the village see and understand their responsibilities, for example within an extended family which draws together thirty-five siblings.

The children also considered what their own responsibility might be to those living in different material conditions. They recognised that the village needed a total of only £3,000 to construct the community library building. Motivated towards social **justice,** the children took the story back to their own families and friends. By their own initiative they raised money by selling toys that people no longer wanted on behalf of the community library – in particular to buy a book binding machine. They raised more than was needed – £312 – enough to put the roof on part of the building.

These children learned about citizenship and the application of moral principles in a different community setting and they took action themselves in response. The project is an example of **education for values-based participation** (Holden and Clough 1998:14). Such an approach is central to this book.

Supporting active learning in citizenship

This book heralds the important principle promoted by John Dewey (1900) that schools have the responsibility to bring democracy into schools and classrooms. The activities in this book support this premise and implementing them may have far reaching consequences for the experience of teachers and learners as they are underpinned by particular pedagogical approaches. These approaches are participatory, open-ended and interactive. They come from an established and radical tradition based on the writings of Paulo Freire (1972) and Carl Rogers (1983). They take as fundamental the tenet that in order to educate children to think and to participate, one must use interactive participatory methods of teaching. The methodology has been developed by the World Studies Trust, Development Education Centres and individuals such as Richardson (1976), Fisher (1980), Fisher and Hicks (1985), Hicks and Steiner (1989) and Pike and Selby (1988). Indeed the sub-title of this book 'Ideas into Action' has been purposefully chosen in recognition of a previous seminal publication of this name.

Rationale for active learning within citizenship education

Citizenship education requires students to:

• Develop confidence to voice own opinions

• Develop skills in recognising the views/experience of other individuals and groups

• Develop skills in critical thinking and in developing arguments

• Develop skills of co-operation and conflict resolution

• Trust in their creative powers

• Develop skills of democratic participation

• Gain experience of taking action for change

Below are some active learning approaches which are modelled in this book.

Examples of active learning approaches

- Small group discussions followed by plenary sessions to develop and synthesise arguments

- Open-ended collaborative enquiries on topical and controversial issues

- Role play, simulations and debates that reflect events in society

- Critically evaluating diverse sources of information

- Direct interaction with community members

- Live correspondence with others living/working inside and outside of the immediate locality

- Entering the lives of others through stories, biographies and other media

- Participating in democratic processes of change.

The content covers the full range of themes identified within the framework for education for citizenship in the National Curriculum for England including:

- social and moral education
- community involvement
- political literacy

It includes sections on what many teachers would see as new dimensions of the curriculum, including:

- conflict resolution and peer group mediation
- involvement in the community
- learning about the citizen and the law
- understanding decision-making through democratic procedures
- awareness of the global community

In each chapter there are outlines for lessons for students aged 7–14 (Key Stage 2 and Key Stage 3). These support teachers who wish to teach citizenship as a discrete area of the curriculum, as well as those who are looking to incorporate it into subject areas. The activities are all based on a common framework which identifies:

- *Purpose:* identifying learning outcomes related to education for citizenship and other subject areas.
- *Preparation:* providing information about resources needed.
- *Procedure:* providing guidance on the content and sequence of the activities, from whole class introductions to group work; providing examples of key questions to encourage discussion and involvement.
- *Plenary:* providing points of focus which will encourage students to analyse their findings and draw conclusions.
- *Possibilities:* providing ideas for follow-up activities.

A significant principle in this book is one that derives from the work of Stenhouse (1980) – that the curriculum is developed and guided best through the intellectual activity of the teacher. Thus each chapter in this book identifies a series of key issues to promote discussion in staff rooms and to inform subsequent development of the activities. Information about recent research findings related to these issues is also included to support students and teachers engaged in academic and enquiry processes. In this way the book is a reference point for the curriculum leader/teacher trainer and also for practitioners involved in evidence-based curriculum development.

Handling controversial issues

A basic tenet of citizenship education is that controversial issues should be included for discussion.

> Controversial issues are important in themselves and to omit informing about and discussing them is to leave a wide and significant gap in the educational experience of young people. (QCA 1998: 56)

We would agree that it is the role of the school to provide opportunities for truthful and honest discussions about points of conflict and agreement that are found in the real world. This means that schools must do more than provide a 'safe haven', as such an ethos may deny children the opportunities to explore relevant topical and political issues. Issues which frequently arise with children relate to the use of drugs, racist incidents, bullying and acts of violence or vandalism in the community. It follows that there will be an increased role for the child to express opinion, discuss, debate and develop ideas during lessons. However this can bring its own problems. Teachers are rightly concerned that their own contributions or those of students in their class may be biased and reflect strongly held opinions which may be difficult to manage.

It is for this reason that the consultative report on Education for Citizenship and the Teaching of Democracy (QCA 1998) includes clear guidance to teachers on the significance of different strategies for managing controversial issues in classrooms. The report recognises the need for balance and careful measures of neutrality on the part of the teacher. Neutrality is recommended as a strategy because the teacher acting as an impartial chair can enable children to extend their thinking skills. The teachers on page 135 in Chapter 7 endorse this, confirming that the children themselves will usually provide balanced opinions. However there are some occasions when the teacher may need to assert a commitment to a value position. For example, the teacher may need to intervene if the democratic process in the classroom has not been sufficient to counter the expression of an anti-social viewpoint (for example a racist opinion) with the effect that individuals in the class or members of the community are left exposed and vulnerable.

Encouraging interculturalism at local and global levels

A recent report by the Commission on the Future of Multi-Ethnic Britain (Runnymede 2000) has identified a series of action points to counter continuing racial discrimination and disadvantage experienced by minority communities. These action points include recommendations for the school curriculum as follows:

> Education for citizenship [should] include human rights principles; skills of deliberation, advocacy and campaigning; open mindedness and tolerance of difference; knowledge of global interdependence; understanding of equality legislation; and opposition to racist beliefs and behaviour. (Runnymede 2000: 149)

In this way, the discussion of virtues earlier in this chapter becomes significant. The relationship between self and collective is again highlighted as an essential aspect of learning to participate as a citizen. In a plural/multicultural society, this involves an extended process of mutuality. Parekh calls for interactive and dynamic relationships or what we could refer to as interculturalism. He argues:

> Since each culture is inherently limited, a dialogue between them is mutually beneficial. It both alerts them to their biases, a gain in itself, and enables them to reduce them and expand their horizon of thought. (Parekh 2000: 336)

There is an agenda here not just for children, but for teachers as well. It is time to see our lives within a plurality of life opportunities. There are opportunities

Rationale for citizenship education

Effective citizens of the twenty-first century will:

- work co-operatively with others

- develop social justice principles to guide own actions

- think in a critical and systemic way

- appreciate and learn from cultural differences

- evaluate problems in the wider community and global context

- resolve conflicts non-violently

- change lifestyles to protect the environment

- recognise and defend human rights

- dare to strive for a fairer future

- participate in democratic politics

Purposes of citizenship education

Schools need a curriculum for citizenship education which:

- provides opportunities for the development of values based on social justice and human rights principles

- encourages respect for different national, religious and ethnic identities and opposition to racist beliefs and behaviour

- links the school with local communities and encourages intercultural learning

- teaches about democracy and the law (past, present and future)

- addresses economic and environmental issues

- provides opportunities for students to set the agenda, to voice their own concerns and to negotiate some areas of learning

- teaches skills of collaborative working, advocacy and campaigning

- models participation in democratic and political processes

- promotes critical thinking and interactive learning

- is realised through the ethos and actions of the school, so that students feel that teachers are fair and that their voices are heard, recognised and acted upon to cross the boundaries of culture and class and the invitation is there to do so. One parent commented in an interview about school and community:

> *I think they [teachers] should get out into the community – what community we have and try to learn what actually is going on. ... Go at it a different way. In all the community events we have, all the little things they have in the community, I have never seen a teacher from the school...* (Clough 1999)

Responding to this kind of invitation could make a difference.

Summary: developing a policy document for citizenship education

The discussion above has identified the essence of the relationship between key values and learning outcomes in citizenship education. Pointers are provided in the handouts to support schools in the process of preparing policy documents for citizenship education. In writing this book we hope to provide guidance for teachers in the fundamental task of assisting children's participation. Such participation can work on many levels but must be informed and premised on recognised virtues and values. We hope that the book brings enjoyment to teachers and learners at the same time as developing further understanding of education for citizenship.

Notes

Handouts 6 and 7 show checklists of learning outcomes for education for citizenship which have been drawn from the National Curriculum. These checklists may be used to:

- identify curriculum subjects which can support this learning
- identify aspects of citizenship education which need to be introduced into the curriculum

We have tended to refer to 'children' when describing activities suitable for the primary school, and 'students' when describing activities suitable for the secondary school, but often the activities are interchangeable and can be adapted for older or younger children/students.

Subject Key

E: English	Ma: Mathematics
Sci: Science	CE: Citizenship Education
H: History	G: Geography
DT: Design and Technology	Mu: Music
RE: Religious Education	MFL: Modern Foreign Languages
PSHE: Personal, Social and Health Education	

Handout 6: education for citizenship – Key Stage 2

Summary of learning objectives for end of Key Stage 2	
Understand and discuss topical matters which affect themselves and society. Express own opinions about such issues	
Recognise their own worth as individuals by identifying positive things about themselves and their achievements	
Face new challenges positively by collecting information, looking for help, making responsible choices and taking action	
Know about the range of jobs carried out by people they know and understand how they can develop skills to make their own contributions in the future	
Understand why rules and laws are made and enforced, why different rules are needed in different situations and how to take part in making/changing rules	
Understand responsibilities and rights at home, in the community and at school and that these can sometimes conflict with each other	
Consider moral and social issues in their own lives, using imagination to understand other people's experience	
Understand what democracy is, and about institutions that support it locally and nationally	
Resolve differences by looking at alternatives, making decisions and explaining choices	
Understand the work of voluntary, community and pressure groups	
Appreciate the range of national, regional, religious and ethnic identities in the United Kingdom	
Understand that resources can be allocated in different ways and that these economic choices affect individuals, communities and the sustainability of the environment	
Explore how the media present information	
Think about people living in other places and times and people with different values and customs	
Realise the nature and consequences of racism, teasing, bullying and aggressive behaviours, and how to respond to them and ask for help	
Recognise and challenge stereotypes	
Understand that differences and similarities between people arise from a number of factors, including cultural, ethnic, racial and religious diversity, gender and disability	

Handout 7: education for citizenship – Key Stage 3

Summary of learning objectives for end of Key Stage 3	
Understand the legal and human rights and responsibilities underpinning society, and basic aspects of the criminal justice system	
Appreciate the diversity of national, regional, religious and ethnic identities in the United Kingdom and the need for mutual respect and understanding	
Know about central and local government, the public services they offer and how they are financed	
Recognise the key characteristics of parliamentary and other forms of government	
Understand the electoral system and the importance of voting	
Know about the work of community-based, national and international voluntary groups	
Appreciate the importance of resolving conflict fairly	
Understand the significance of the media in society	
Recognise the world as a global community, and the political, economic, environmental and social implications of this, and the role of the EU, the Commonwealth and the United Nations	
Think about topical political, spiritual, moral, social and cultural issues and events by analysing information and its sources	
Justify orally and in writing a personal opinion about such issues, problems or events	
Contribute to group and exploratory class discussions and take part in debates	
Use imagination to consider other people's experience and be able to think about and express and explain views that are not their own	
Negotiate, decide and take part responsibly in both school and community-based activities	
Reflect on the process of participating	

Democratic Processes: School Councils, School Parliaments and Peer Mediation

Democracy is best learned in a democratic setting where participation is encouraged, where views can be expressed openly and discussed, where there is freedom of expression for pupils and teachers, and where there is fairness and justice. (Council of Europe 1985)

Our [school] parliament is more controlled than the real one. (Boy, aged 11)

Introduction

It is often maintained that schools are mini-societies that reflect the world at large and that learning to live in these will prepare children for adult life. On this premise many schools have established school councils, where representatives from each class come together in a council of students, teachers and others involved in the running of the school. Some schools have opted for school parliaments, and others have peer mediation schemes where students are responsible for helping their peers find their own solutions to problems (often in the playground). Behind all these schemes lies a belief in students having a right to voice their opinions and to be actively involved in the school community.

Key issues

Voice and agency

How can we give all students a 'voice'? How can we give them a sense of 'agency', of their own ability to achieve change? How can we make schools a more equitable place? Will more power for students mean less power for teachers? Will it help raise standards?

Democratic processes

How can we model democratic processes in school? Is it possible for students to learn about negotiation, debate and compromise by taking part in the running of the school? Is it possible to teach about parliamentary processes by recreating these in a school setting?

The role of students in conflict resolution

How can we make the playground environment safer, with less bullying and conflict? Can we use students' abilities as mediators to help others resolve conflict? Is the teacher abdicating responsibility if students are trained to use peer mediation? How will this affect standards of behaviour?

Recent research findings

Voice and agency

With the Universal Declaration of Human Rights (1948) and the subsequent United Nations Convention on the Rights of the Child (1989), there has been recognition that children have a right to be listened to and that their concerns should be taken into account. Furthermore research has indicated that taking on board the views of children can contribute to the raising of standards in that children become more motivated if they see themselves as having a voice in their own learning and in the institutions in which they spend their day (Trafford 1993). Davies suggests that there is less disaffection and lower exclusion rates in schools which listen to what students, as the school's customers, have to say about improving their school (Davies 1998).

One way of giving children a voice is to have a school council. Rudduck maintains that councils work best if they are part of school-wide democratic practice. She points to the danger of councils becoming 'a way of formalising and channelling students' criticisms – an exercise in damage limitation rather than an opportunity for constructive consultation' (Rudduck et al. 1997). Too often, she says, councils are only involved in discussions about dinners, toilets and uniform. If students are to feel they really have a voice, the council should be a vehicle for student participation in major decision-making processes, allowing them to exercise rights and responsibilities and contribute to the school community. Real participation will involve the transfer of some power from management to student, which for Harber (1998) is the mark of a democratic school. But Rowe (1996) acknowledges that giving students a voice is not as simple as it may seem. There may be conflict over what the parents, the governors and the students want or there may be views which conflict with teachers' professional judgement. What if pupils (or parents) were to object to the school's anti-racist policies or wanted to replace a curriculum area to which the school felt a strong commitment? Nonetheless, if the school is to model democratic processes then there must be a place for dissenting views to be aired even if the rights of the management of the school to run it according to its own principles ultimately prevail.

Democratic processes

Whilst many advocate school councils because they wish to give pupils a forum for voicing their opinions and concerns, for some, such councils serve a different purpose: namely to mirror or model the democratic structures of society 'so that students learn experientially what being part of a democratic community really means' (Rowe 1996:10). Education for citizenship requires that pupils learn about democratic processes, about parliament, about debate and decision making and it is suggested that as schools are mini-societies, they are well placed to teach about such processes. This has been seen at its most successful where schools run their own parliaments (QCA 2000), which enable children to learn about proposing and opposing motions, voting and representation. Indeed increasing the 'political literacy' of young people is one of the key aims of the new citizenship curriculum.

The role of children in conflict resolution

More recently there has been a move to involve students in situations beyond the formal setting of the school council or parliament. Many schools are now involved in peer mediation programmes whereby students are trained to help their peers find their own solutions to problems through processes which are based on non-violent conflict resolution. Such processes (like school councils) take as fundamental the rights of children to be listened to, to express their opinions and to have their views considered.

Peer mediation, although under-researched, has yielded evidence (Griffith 1996; Stacey 1996; Tyrrell and Farrell 1995) that highlights its potential in the U.K. Peer mediators seem proficient in developing the skills required and the process of mediating has a positive impact on their own self-esteem, locus of control and interpersonal skills. Benefits to the school include the prevention of major conflict, as many problems which may seem small and 'petty' to teachers can be prevented by peer mediators who help students take responsibility for resolving their own conflicts. Peer mediation is most successful in reducing destructive conflict in schools where there is a co-operative culture and a whole school approach, where teachers are prepared to allow students to develop and practise skills in regulating their own behaviour. As with school councils and school parliaments, there are often problems of continuity when children transfer from primary to secondary. Highly skilled students may not given the opportunities to practise their skills and may feel frustrated and disempowered. Conversely, where there are good schemes in place, new students need to be sufficiently grounded in the processes to use the scheme (Sellman 2000).

Practice in schools

Effective school councils

A school council is an elected body, consisting of representatives from each class (councillors) and a chairperson who is usually an adult (teacher, governor, etc.). It is set up to provide students with a voice and to help in the smooth running of the school. The councillors bring suggestions or requests from their class or year group to the meeting which are then discussed and either rejected or accepted. Suggestions which are accepted are then forwarded for action to the most appropriate body. Councillors feed back to their class or year group on the outcomes.

Those who benefit from a school council:

1   The individual students who are councillors: increased self-esteem, insight into running of school, increased social skills.

2   The student body as a whole: having a voice through their councillors, improvements in conditions for students.

3   The ethos of a school: improved relationships between staff and pupils, co-operation rather than conflict.

4   The staff: task of senior management made more effective as a result of input of information from students, students gain more understanding of reasons for management decisions.

(Rowe 1996)

Issues to consider

Getting the support of teachers

Teachers need to be convinced of the value of the council and allow discussion of relevant council matters in their lessons, as well as considering any issues raised which relate to their own teaching or learning environment. You need to ensure that teachers do not see the council as a marginal event. As one student said, it's 'like a black hole – they just say "we'll look into it" and you never hear any more' (Rowe 1996: 11).

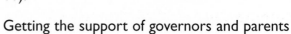

Getting the support of governors and parents

It is important to explain the benefits of a school council to governors as, for one thing, requests from students may come their way. Governors will need to know how the council will help meet the requirements for citizenship education, and will benefit the school in other ways.

You will need the support of parents or some may worry that if their children are councillors the time taken will adversely affect their school work. Explaining the rationale behind a school council also provides an opportunity to talk about the

importance of giving children a voice, valuing their opinion and encouraging debate. It is also a chance to explain education for citizenship and its importance.

Communication

Councillors must have sufficient time before meetings to ascertain what issues the class or year group want to be taken to the council and to report back afterwards. Circle time in primary schools and PSME lessons or year group meetings in secondary school often provide an appropriate forum for this. It is also important that meetings are minuted to ensure that feedback is accurate. Some schools have a minute book, others have a council noticeboard.

The chair

The role of the chair is important. It needs to be someone with status: either the head teacher or deputy, a governor, head boy/girl, so that they can ensure that matters are carried forward quickly and with observable outcomes.

Frequency and timing of meetings

This is crucial. If they happen in break time or after school, there will be few volunteers and this sends a message about the council's marginalisation. Ideally it should be run either in PSHE (secondary) or members should be taken from lessons on a rotation basis so that the same lesson is not missed. Some primary schools have found silent reading sessions or hymn practice a good time for council meetings.

A budget

Many primary schools give the council a small budget which can be used for items such as refreshments and a noticeboard. Some secondary schools give a larger budget which can be used to address some of the students' requests.

There are many organisations and publications to help you get started, and two teachers below talk about their work with councils. If you already have a council you may wish to consider the following:

Developing the work of the council

Some councils extend their work to include behaviour problems. In one school individual behaviour problems are brought to the council, who may then decide to send for that child if their behaviour is persistently challenging. In some cases, the council has asked to meet the parents of that child. Another primary school has instigated a 'listening bench' where two members of the school council take it in turns to sit on a special bench at playtimes and act as 'listeners' for those who have problems or who are lonely. Similarly, in a large secondary school, members of the school council are available each lunchtime for 'anyone to come up and if they have any problems to talk to us', in an effort to stop bullying in the first year of the school. Not all work focuses on behaviour: one secondary school council monitors homework set and puts this on a special board so that anyone absent can find out what is to be done. (Davies 1998)

19

Case study: running a school council in a large secondary school – a teacher talks

How does the council operate?

Each year group has its own council, made up of representatives from every tutor group, and each year council from Years 7–10 sends four representatives to the college council. Year 11 have six representatives because they run the college council: they are chair, vice chair and secretary and they are responsible totally for running the meeting. The sixth form have their own college council and send the student presidents to the college council meeting, but they don't chair it. It's chaired from Year 11. We do this because we want to give Year 11 responsibility in preparation for the extra responsibilities of sixth form.

The college council meets once a half term, as do the year councils. The year councils are timetabled to meet just before the college council and so they feed in issues that have been discussed. The meeting follows a formal agenda and normally it is a standard form of apologies, minutes of last meeting, matters arising. This shows what follow-up has been done or not done and what responses there have been to various issues.

College council is held during lesson time so those students are allowed out of lessons. That's a real privilege and they see that as such, although the year councils are at lunchtime, so they do have to give up some of their own time. And if you are elected on to the committee you have to do some work – the secretary has to write the minutes for example. In the past college councils have also been given money to spend: about £500, a significant sum. One year they decided to spend it on clocks in every classroom, but that was their decision.

What is the council's main role?

At one level it's very much about 'We want better toilets, we want better things in the tuck shop'. Recently they were very unhappy with the length of the queue for the refectory and so we provided a separate service for snacks and that certainly made a difference. But it also relates to outside bodies. For example at the last meeting we had the librarian from Tavistock library who asked the college council to do a survey into reading habits and what young people would want in the new library which is being built in Tavistock by Devon County Council. They did this. They set up a working party and devised a questionnaire which went out to a sample of students and is now back with the library. Another example is when we were approached by the Best Value play committee of the town council : they wanted youngsters to take part in a play sub-committee. We agreed that they should hold this in college, so they had a formal sub committee of the town council here with students taking an equal part and that was found to be very useful. In a way, this is citizenship in action because it's having a body you can use when approached by outside organisations.

The other thing that we have done this term is the United Kingdom Youth Parliament. We held a formal competition amongst the members of the college council and having given a speech, three were selected (by their peers) to represent us. Actually the boy who came first is going to London to be in the National Youth Parliament in February. He's only 12, he was competing largely with sixth formers, but he was so confident and that's all come out of having to speak all the way through from his year council to the college council. So that's a real practical outcome – people can see that the year council feeds the college council which feeds to something else which is much bigger.

What is your role?

I always attend as vice-principal but I attend 'ex officio' almost, I am not there to lead at all, I'm just there to speak if asked to. Being quiet for most of the time is quite hard for a teacher but actually it's very interesting to see young people becoming empowered...At the last council there were some issues that were raised by younger students which were being answered by the older students. It was so interesting to hear them say 'Look, you can't ask for that, that's absolutely ridiculous'. It's so much better coming from them – that's a real bonus, when students start seeing organisational things from an adult perspective.

What about when you have to say 'No'?

It would depend on the circumstances but it would never come from me at the meeting. What I try to do is take it to the appropriate person and they are required to write back to me. I will then report back. Of course sometimes there is a 'No'. One request was about the changing rooms being crowded and could new rooms be built? 'No', we said, we have to live with what we've got. More lockers were requested, but actually they answered that themselves saying new ones would be too expensive and there was nowhere to put them. But we don't often say 'No' in that sense. As long as you can say why you are saying 'No', – and it's got to be a good explanation because you've got to respect them – then they understand.

With thanks to Graham Stoate, Vice-Principal, Tavistock College.

Case study: introducing a school council in a village primary school – a teacher's account

The deputy head teacher started the assembly by explaining that too often teachers were unaware of children's views and that if they knew more about what children thought, the school would be a better place. She then introduced the basic idea of democracy, and how this involves listening to people's views before decisions are made. She had a large poster which illustrated the main groups of people in the education system, including children, who make decisions about how schools are run.

She then explained

1   *We're going to plan more class time for you to talk about school issues – so that we can get to know what you think about being in our school AND*

2   *We're going to set up a school council. A school council is a group of pupils who will work with teachers at making West Hill Primary School a better place to work and to play. They will help let everyone know what pupils in other classes think about important school issues.*

How it will work:

Your teacher will plan more time for you to talk about school issues in your own class. Then ... you will elect two people, a boy and a girl, to be your class councillor. It will be the job of each class councillor to bring the ideas of their class to the school council meeting. And there will be me. I'll be at the meetings to help out and in the beginning to be the chairperson. But I won't stay the chairperson for long, Once the fourteen class councillors are confident and get used to running their own meetings, they'll decide on their own chairperson, vice chairperson, secretary and even treasurer!

Being a class councillor will be a very important job for three reasons:

• *because they will tell everyone at the meeting what their OWN class thinks about important school issues*

• *because they will then make plans and work on them together, to improve our school*

• *because they will report back to their own class on everything that the council discussed at the meeting.*

Your teacher has planned some time, either today or tomorrow, for you to get into groups and discuss and write down answers to this question:

> *What are some of the things we would like adults to listen to about school life here at West Hill School?*

This weekend, I will take them all home, sort them out and let you know on Monday, about all the different ideas. Then next week, I'll have a special meeting with some interested Year 6 children to discuss and plan ways to help you decide and vote for your two class councillors.

So ... like I said at the beginning of the assembly ... This is a BIG idea, for us!

Thanks to Lynne Carre, for sharing her notes for the initial assembly to start a school council at West Hill Primary School.

I would like to be elected on to the School Council because:

I think the idea of a School Council is a very good idea.

I would like to be part of a team.

I would like everyone to have their say.

I am willing to put time and effort into it.

I would like to put forward ideas and see them happen.

(Year 6 child, West Hill School)

I would like the person I vote for to be:

brave

someone who doesn't fidget

polite

a good thinker

a good summariser

calm

fair

sensible

a clear speaker

good at listening

(Year 3: the qualities required
of a councillor, West Hill School)

Ideas for the School Council to discuss:

- a pet in each class
- a patch on the field where we can run and jump
- more colourful classrooms
- no school clothes on Fridays
- more animal story books
- girls to talk to boys more and no teasing
- a school newspaper
- more languages (Italian and German)
- more sports facilities

(Year 5, West Hill School)

Effective school parliaments

While a school parliament has many similarities to a school council, the emphasis is more on learning about democratic processes, including the roles of ministers in parliament, and debating issues from a for/against perspective. There is less emphasis on dealing with behaviour management. The main differences are:

• all students are members of parliament

• instead of councillors, there are elected ministers, each with a brief

• there is a prime minister, a leader of the opposition and a speaker

• each issue is subject to a debate which looks at both sides of the argument

• voting on any issue involves the whole school (as the parliament).

Benefits of a school parliament

There are additional benefits to those of a council:

1   for the individual students who are ministers: experience of having to oppose (or propose) a motion they may themselves not support.

2   for the student body as a whole: modelling the processes of parliament, so that students understand debating, how ministers work towards their brief, how every issue has two sides: allowing greater student participation (than councils) in that the parliament meetings involve the whole school with all students able to vote on issues.

Issues to consider

In addition to the issues to consider for a council you will need to consider the time which will be needed for this. As with a school council, there needs to be dedicated lesson time so that each class can decide what issues they wish to put forward to the ministers for debate, but in addition a parliament will also need time in whole school assemblies when the issues are debated and votes are cast.

How to get started

As with a school council, you will need the support of staff and governors. In addition to the arguments in support of school councils, you can add that running a parliament will support the current requirement that students learn 'what democracy is, and the basic institutions that support it' (QCA 2000). When introducing the idea to students there may not be a neighbouring school parliament to draw on, but you may be able to get your local MP to come and explain the important work a parliament does. The following case study shows the steps taken by one school to set up a parliament and reports on the opinions of the current ministers, three years on.

Case study: Alverton Primary School Parliament

Background and rationale

The idea for a school parliament originated four years ago from an Australian teacher (from Deniliquin South School, New South Wales) who was in this primary school in the south-west of England on a teacher exchange. The parliament was instigated in 1997 and is going from strength to strength. It was recently cited in the QCA guidelines for citizenship as an example of good practice (QCA 2000).

The aims of the parliament are to:

- familiarise children with the mechanics and procedures of national and local government

- give children an opportunity to speak publicly, to organise agendas and motions for debate and to listen carefully to the views of others

- give children a sense of responsibility and involvement in decisions which affect their school.

The structure

There are ten ministers, a speaker, a prime minister and a leader of the opposition, all from Year 6. They have the following roles:

- a prime minister (proposing motions)

- a leader of the opposition (opposing the motions)

- a speaker (keeping everyone in order)

- two ministers for the environment and health (looking after the school grounds, introducing incentives to improve the school environment)

- two ministers for finance and library (liaising with librarian, monitoring tuck shop, money-raising incentives)

- two ministers for sport and recreation (i/c sports cupboard, liaising with PE co-ordinator)

- two ministers for arts and music (helping with play sets, giving out certificates for artist of the month, sorting out music)

- two ministers for media and communication (writing letters as needed, collecting school news for column for local paper).

There are meetings of ministers and the link teacher once every couple of weeks and whole school parliaments two to three times each term.

The process

Summer term:

Year 5 pupils who wish to be elected write their election speeches, saying which post they would like. These brief speeches are delivered over a week of assemblies. Year 2–6 children vote on ballot papers and the results are posted. The outgoing cabinet and link teacher have the final say on which ministers get which jobs. At the final parliament of the summer term the outgoing ministers hand over their badges in an 'inauguration' ceremony.

Autumn term: preparations for the first parliament session

Two weeks before:

Initial meeting with ministers and link teacher to discuss the first session. Each minister will be asked to give a short speech concerning his/her area of responsibility. Each has a 'buddy' teacher with whom to discuss this.

The week before:

Each class has a discussion to decide what motions they want to put forward. The class teacher facilitates this discussion and helps prioritise the motions so that only one goes forward from each class. Ministers come round to collect the motions. The prime minister, speaker, leader of the opposition and link teacher meet and select three of the motions put forward for the next parliamentary session. Prime minister and leader of the opposition then prepare speeches for and against these motions. All classes receive an agenda listing the three motions.

On the Monday or Tuesday of the week of the meeting:

Final meeting of ministers and link teacher to check speeches/reports, etc. Class teachers run through the motions with their class and open up the debate. This allows children to practise airing their views.

Thursday afternoon:

Year 6 prepare the hall. Classes arrive then ministers are summoned, with 'all stand for the ministers' from the speaker. Ministers file in and children sit. The speaker opens the session of the parliament by asking each pair of ministers to give their reports, followed by the reading of the first motion. The prime minister then speaks for the motion and the leader of the opposition against. The speaker then opens the debate to the floor. Children who wish to make a contribution stand and are chosen by the speaker. It is the speaker's job to encourage and order this process. Children are then asked to vote for or against the motion (heads down, hands up). If a count is necessary the prime minister and leader of the opposition do this and hand the results to the speaker, who then announces whether the motion has been passed or not. The process is then repeated for the next two motions. The speaker then calls for the parliament to be closed, the ministers file out and the children leave.

Follow-up:

Motions which have been passed are then discussed at the fortnightly meetings with ministers. Either the ministers are able to take action themselves or the motions are taken to staff meetings and discussed, or to governors' meetings, depending on the motion. The regular meetings with ministers allow agreed decisions/points for action to be monitored and chased up.

The teachers' views:

The teachers commented that it was important to encourage the children to look at a broad range of issues including:

- the environment (e.g. recycling)

- resources for the school

- road safety

- special events, school clubs

This was one way of maintaining enthusiasm and helped ensure that the same issues did not come up again and again. They stressed that most of the issues raised were usually quite uncontroversial and could be taken forward for discussion and possible implementation. However, if they were problematic it was important that they were not dismissed by staff out of hand, but that they were discussed thoroughly with ministers before being rejected. Children needed to feel that the effort they put into the parliament was not a waste of time and hence there needed to be a commitment by the staff to meet requests that were reasonable and practicable. In fact 80% of motions passed so far have been acted upon.

One commented:

> *We have found the parliament to be an opportunity to model good behaviour in a public domain. Children know that they cannot interrupt each other or call out and even the youngest children learn about taking turns and respecting the views of others.*

The children's views:

An interview with the prime minister (PM), speaker (S) and leader of the opposition (LO) indicated strong support for their parliament. There had been physical improvements such as locks on the toilet doors ('before we had to put pencils in the locks') and at the summer fête ministers had run a stall to raise money for goals in the top playground. The PM gave another example:

> *Like the new pond ... it was just a square sort of thing that had netting over it and it was really boring so there was a motion that we should have a new pond and that got passed and now we've got a pond with a fountain and everything round it has been changed.*

They said that while most motions got passed, this was not automatic as they had 'to be passed on to the governors and if they decide that that's OK and we've got enough money to pay for it then it gets done'. Sometimes they did have to 'chase things up' if what they had agreed to did not happen. All three agreed that they had benefited personally from being ministers. 'You get more and more confident at speaking out ... before I did parliament I was so nervous', said S. In addition they liked being 'more involved in how the school is running and the library and finance ministers are more involved in the money and how the library is run'. They admitted that often the most difficult role was the leader of the opposition as he had to speak against the motion when often he was in agreement with it. LO cited the example of the motion for a fizzy drinks machine where he had to argue that it would cost too much and that 'fizzy drinks hype people up'. Even so, the motion was carried.

There was general agreement that being a minister took up a lot of time. They had to report back on motions, 'sort out files and stuff' and write the speeches. This could take 'about half an hour a day' but they helped each other out and liaised over the phone. When asked if they would vote as adults, they all agreed that they would and were confident that having their own parliament had helped them understand how the English parliament works. They were not, however, that impressed with the latter. Their recent visit to the Houses of Parliament to see 'real' ministers at work had left them rather sceptical:

> *It was good seeing the important people but the actual debate was, well ... boring. (LO)*

> *Our parliament is more controlled than the real one and more sensible. (S)*

They were optimistic that the school council at their secondary school would provide them with a voice and were keen to be involved in that. The PM concluded:

I'd just like to say parliament is really good for this school and I think every school should have one.

With thanks to Tessa Garland, PGCE student, University of Exeter,
Carole Webster and Rick Gill, teachers at Alverton School.

27

Effective peer mediation

Peer mediation is a process by which mediators are trained to help students find their own solutions to problems and conflicts in the school environment. They are usually identifiable by a badge or pin, and have a 'base' from which to operate. They are taught the specific skills required (often by an outside agency) and are given very clear guidance on the processes involved. They are supported by link staff – either teachers or meal-time assistants.

Those who benefit from peer mediation are

1   The individual students who are mediators: increased self-esteem, locus of control and interpersonal skills.

2   The student body as a whole: having trained mediators to call on, having a safer playground, learning models of non-violent resolution of conflict.

3   The ethos of a school: improved atmosphere out of lessons reflected in the classroom, fewer major disruptive conflicts as minor conflicts are prevented from escalating.

4   Playground supervisors: having support in the playground to help children sort out their own problems.

5   The staff: less time spent sorting out petty squabbles or arguments, more teaching time, models of conflict resolution can be used in the classroom.

Issues to consider when embarking on a peer mediation programme

The choice of mediators

It is important that peer mediators are seen as a representative sample of the school population. There should be an even representation of all groups in the school. It is also important that students volunteer to be peer mediators, after which they should be selected by election. Training slightly younger pupils is often worthwhile as their skills will be retained and developed.

The choice of trainer

There is some temptation to train peer mediators from within the school. However, peer mediation is a complex process and its training is best done by specialised agencies. These will work with a group of young people in forming a group, priming them with the interpersonal skills needed and setting up the scheme. They will also provide continued support in running the scheme and refresher courses. In time, older students and experienced staff should be able to train younger students with reduced assistance.

The role of the teachers and playground supervisors

Usually a link teacher is appointed. It is also crucial to involve meal-time assistants or playground supervisors as they need to work with the students, not by a separate set of rules. There will also be some problems too complex for peer mediators to deal with, and adults need to be at hand to help. The mediators need to know when it is appropriate to seek adult help.

The frequency and timing of meetings of mediators

When the meetings take place is crucial. If they happen in break time or after school, there will be few volunteers and this sends a message about its marginalisation. Ideally meetings should happen on a rotation basis so that the same lesson is not missed.

How to get started

As with school councils and parliaments, it is important to have the support of staff, pupils, governors and parents. Again the introduction of a new scheme needs to be taken step by step and if there are schools who have successful schemes in place, it would be useful to invite in a representative. However, as noted in the 'role of the trainer' above, peer mediation is a complex process and initial training is best done by specialised agencies. There are a number of training bodies nationwide, with some contacts given in the Resources section.

A trainer of peer mediators writes:

> Before peer mediators are selected, some work is done with the whole school or a year group in developing skills in affirmation, communication, co-operation as well as knowledge and understanding of and problem solving approaches to conflict. These key skills are essential pre-requisites to a peer mediation scheme being successful as they create a pool of potential clients with the skills and attitudes to make best use of a peer mediation scheme. Later, peer mediators will be chosen and additional training given. The format for both this and previous training is commonly delivered via circle time activities. The group works together to develop and implement a group contract for the sessions. This uses their ideas to regulate the group and provides an understanding of the first step of peer mediation: agreeing and working to voluntary protocols.

> Additional work is done on understanding the dynamics of conflicts, particularly the role of relationships in pursuing personal goals. This is supported with practising key skills in listening, repeating the facts and facilitating disputants into offering and agreeing their own solutions to a problem. Some work is always done on handling difficulties in peer mediation. In many of the schools in which I have encountered peer mediation schemes, they appear to have been very successful in both developing the skills of those trained and in having an impact on reducing instances of destructive conflict. However, this has only been the case in schools prepared to change their school organisation and culture rather than schools who specifically want to change the behaviour of a problem class. It has to be part of a whole school initiative, where all staff are prepared to endorse the scheme and allow pupils opportunities to regulate their own behaviour. Peer mediation should not detract from teacher–pupil conflicts and therefore needs to be part of a whole school process towards creating a more open, co-operative and democratic school.

> (Edward Sellman trains peer mediators for the West Midlands Quaker Peace Education Project. His interest in training peer mediators arose from a concern that schools didn't allow students many positive experiences of constructive conflict and a voice in resolving their own disputes. He is currently evaluating work in schools as part of a PhD at the School of Education, University of Birmingham.)

Case study: North Prospect Primary School

Peer mediation was introduced to this inner-city school by a new Head who felt that 'the wrong sort of behaviours had crept into the school', that the children did not seem to have 'self-discipline ... and those values about education and respect for other people that you just take for granted'. He saw peer mediation as a chance to improve inter-personal skills:

> It's not just about the school ethos and maintaining order in the school, it's about transferable skills. If some of these children are able to resolve conflict situations or let's face it, learn to listen and hear other people's points of view and respect that and respond accordingly, then it's a very valuable experience.

Initial training was provided by an outside agency and there is now a regular programme of training and support. Two children from Years 3, 4 and 6 act as peer mediators with Year 2 children being trained, so that in Year 3 they can be mediators for the Key Stage I classes. The Head commented that 'some of the best mediators are the children who have had the most problems'. However, all mediators must be supported so that they do not become 'isolated by peers or subject to unpleasant comment' and their parents need to know what their children are doing to reassure them that they are not at risk. Interviews with some of the mediators indicate their understanding of their roles. A Year 2 child explained:

> Mediators keep the problem small ... You can sort it out because you can ask that person if they're OK to say sorry. If they are guilty and jealous you can say you don't need to feel guilty and jealous. They can say sorry to each other, they can play with each other ... And if they can't be friends then they have to agree to be nice to each other ... They can't pick fights.

Year 6 children were able to elaborate further:

> G   They come to you with this problem they tell us, and once you think you've got the problem you discuss it with your partner and you say is this your problem? And if they say, yes, then you say, right, I'm putting it in this magic box and I'll keep it with me.

> B   Then you say right, it's brainstorm time and you ask them if they've got any ideas what they could do to make the problem work and they'll give you like seven or eight ideas and you repeat the ideas over and see what one they want to pick. And if they agree, we'll try it out for about a week until say next week ... Then they come back to you and you say has it worked and if they say `Yes' then we say, `OK I'm glad you've come to us, thank you'.

> G   This is what our trainer told me, mediators stay in the middle, listen to both sides, make life fair and build a bridge.

As part of this case study, parents were also interviewed. One mother confided that even after 12 months she was still 'very nervous' about her Year 5 daughter being a mediator because of what was involved, but nonetheless agreed with other parents that playtimes were better:

> A lot of them felt that they weren't being listened to or they were being pushed away ... Instead of them running to adults where they got dismissed ... now they got these children that they can go to who will listen to them, even if it is stupid, they will talk to them ... They've got somebody on their wavelength, not an adult saying sort it out, you know – 'girls' stuff' and that.

Inevitably there are still problems which need to be resolved. Some children commented that 'the dinner ladies' still send children 'to the corner of the playground, not to us', but they were confident the Head would sort this out. Some staff were less convinced than the children of the value of the system, but all agreed with the Head that 'the school is better, there is less fighting, less arguing'. Finally it needs to be said that peer mediation alone cannot turn round a school. There is also a strong emphasis on social and moral education in this school and it uses other methods of getting children involved in and taking more responsibility for their school, such as school captains and an active school council.

> With thanks to Chris Watts, the staff, pupils and parents of North Prospect Primary School.

Extending Language and Literacy

3

The delight on the children's faces when I was reading the story was wonderful. They were waiting on every breath – there was so much anticipation. They loved the fact that the story was from Greece and they could see the real Greek letters. (Student teacher, using a translated Greek story alongside the original as part of the literacy hour)

If it's a fun thing that you do you're more likely to remember it and take it in, if it's an interesting thing, instead of just working out of text books which is boring and you forget it as soon as you've left the room. (Underachieving boy, aged 13, talking about what makes a good English lesson)

Introduction

Central to citizenship education is the fostering of the independent judgement of the child so that he/she is able to make informed decisions about current moral and ethical issues. The programme of study for citizenship (DfEE/QCA 1999) requires that students learn the skills needed to justify themselves orally and in writing about such issues and that they learn how to consider other people's experiences. Linked to this is an understanding of the significance of the media and its role in shaping values. Thus the requirements of citizenship education dovetail well with those of the English curriculum where pupils must be taught about the power of media, persuasive language, how to respond critically to the views of others and to appreciate the value of other cultures and traditions.

Key issues

Making meaning through language

How can we help students celebrate the diversity of language? How can we help them to understand that language is constantly evolving? How can we give students the skills to analyse persuasive language and to use language persuasively? How can we ensure that all students are given an equal chance to express their opinions and contribute to classroom debate?

Media literacy

How can we help students to appreciate the significance of the media in our society? How can we help them to look critically at media images? How can we use media education to raise issues about fair representation of minority groups?

The contribution of literature

How can we increase students' understanding of the world through the use of texts from other countries and cultures? How can use literature to explore identity? How can we use fiction and non-fiction to help students understand current moral and ethical issues?

Recent research findings

Making meaning through language

It has long been held that children's construction of meaning is conducted through their use and development of language (Epstein 1993). Talk, just as much as listening and observing, has been accepted as an important part of the learning process. If this is so, then there are two areas central to citizenship education and English. First, we must help students to understand the power of language to persuade, to harm, to perpetuate prejudice and their own role in using language sensitively. Second, there is an ongoing debate about equality of access to talk in the classroom. Studies have confirmed that most talk is teacher dominated with students being passive respondents for a large proportion of the time (Grugeon *et al.* 1998). There is little evidence to show that teachers' questions stimulate thought and discussion; in fact often the answers the teacher requires will be found in the lesson and thus real world experiences or analogies are not relevant (Edwards and Mercer 1987). Furthermore, detailed case studies have shown that when the teacher does involve students in whole class discussions, boys, or more specifically a sub-set of boys, dominate the discussion (Arnot *et al.* 1998). If this is the case then the English teacher trying to facilitate a democratic classroom needs to consider the nature and style of questioning and participation.

Media literacy

Young people today are bombarded by the media. Television, radio, newspapers, magazines and the internet are in most homes. If students are to be critically and politically aware citizens, they must be able to evaluate the contribution of the media to our society (Beck 1992). This will include an understanding of the ways in which the media reaffirms or challenges images of cultures, countries and peoples of the North and South. Midwinter (1994) refers to the work on children's perceptions of Africa, carried out in the late 1980s after extensive media coverage of famine and suffering. Their perceptions were found to be stereotyped, narrow and mainly negative. Africa was seen as 'an isolated hungry continent' and Europe as 'the generous benefactor' (Midwinter 1994: 119). Midwinter calls for media education which allows students the opportunity to examine a range of images, asking such questions as: Who has produced this?

Why? What is its purpose? This will begin the process of media literacy which aims to develop students' critical awareness of the process and purpose of image construction.

The English curriculum provides opportunities for media education which link with citizenship. The literacy hour in primary schools requires children to evaluate newspaper articles, to look for bias and to be able to understand persuasive writing (DfEE 1998). At secondary level, students 'should be taught how meaning is conveyed in texts that include print, images and sometimes sound, how choice of form, layout and presentation contribute to effect, and how the nature and purpose of media products influence content and meaning' (DfEE/QCA 1999: 50). Examining current images in newspapers and on television, examining bias and understanding persuasive writing, all link directly to citizenship education.

The contribution of literature

Texts which extend the English curriculum to include citizenship education relate to issues of democracy, justice, social and moral concerns, and reflect our culturally diverse society. Such texts have a major part to play in enriching children's understanding of the human condition. Not only can they provide an insight into the lives of others, they can also provide the focus for discussion of controversial issues, and of moral and ethical issues. Spurgeon (1998) writes of the value of fiction for raising awareness of race, alternative visions of society and issues of belonging. He warns, however, that students bring their own cultural background and prejudices to the texts which may or may not be modified by the teaching strategy employed. Work on such sensitive themes, he concludes, needs to be tackled across the school and not just left to the English teacher.

Both Wood and Richardson (1992) and Burns and Lamont (1995) remind us of the emotional power of story, how it can challenge our values and help us enter other worlds. They advocate a number of different approaches to story, using fables, poems and parables alongside non-fiction to awaken the senses and provide us with a heritage of global literature.

Activities

Using images: what do you see?

Purpose

- To help students understand how images in the media can be used and misused to provide information and provoke emotive responses (CE, E)

- To develop skills of observation and critical analysis (CE, E)

- To understand how meaning is conveyed through texts and images (E)

- To understand how audiences and readers choose and respond to media (E)

Preparation

You will need:

- strips of paper, pens and glue

- pins or tape to attach pictures to the wall

- five or six pictures or photographs from magazines or newspapers (try to choose pictures which can be interpreted in different ways).

Procedures

Pin or tape the pictures to the wall. Give pairs of students strips of plain paper and ask them to look at each picture in turn and then to write two alternative headlines, one positive and one negative, on separate pieces of paper. When everyone is ready, stick the headlines under the pictures. Compare the headlines.

Plenary

- How many different interpretations were there of each picture?

- Did different people see different things in the same picture?

- When you read newspapers or magazines, which do you look at first, the captions or the pictures?

- Do pictures always tell the truth or just some of the truth?

- How do editors use language and images to convey information and arouse emotions?

Possibilities

Follow-up work could focus on one particular aspect of using images and text, e.g. looking at charity appeals, looking at advertisements. Students could try their own persuasive writing for these areas. More work could be done on newspaper images comparing, for example, how different newspapers treat the same news item. The enquiry can be focused by choosing a topical news item, e.g. how asylum seekers are portrayed, how football violence is reported. This will allow further in-depth discussion of how the media portrays images of people and events.

Possibilities plus

Making the news

Give each group of between four and five children a scenario (e.g. baby rescued from burning house, refugees caught entering Britain, racist attack on young girl, new electric car unveiled, councillors agree local bypass to be built). Each group then acts out their scenario, observed by the others who are all 'reporters' and make notes on what they see. Groups then take it in turns to present one of the scenarios they observed as an early evening news bulletin (using a large frame to represent the TV). One member of the group is the news reader. The rest of the class (and the original actors) comment on how fair and accurate this depiction was, referring to their 'reporters' notes. The process is repeated until all scenarios have been presented as news bulletins and discussed.

These activities were adapted from 'What do you see'
in All Different All Equal, *an Education pack produced*
by the European Youth Centre, Council of Europe.

Celebrations?

Birthday cards can also be a useful source of images for challenging stereotypes. You will need lots of examples of birthday cards and other cards (e.g. 'congratulations on the new baby' which you can collect from children and friends). Get the children to sort the cards into groups. Discussion: What images are usually found on boys' cards? On girls' cards? On grandmothers' cards? Do all girls like dolls, flowers? Do all boys like cars, football? Do all grannies have grey hair and knit? Do theirs? How many cards show black people? See the poem 'Happy Birthday Dilroy' in John Agard's 'I Din Do Nuttin'. How did this black boy feel receiving cards with pictures of white children? The children could then design their own cards based on people they know (e.g. sister who climbs trees, granny who plays bingo, does yoga) or cards reflecting our culturally diverse society.

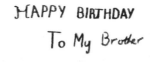

A birthday card for my little brother who likes to play house under the kitchen table. Ahmed, aged 8.

Nelson Mandela:
Different perspectives on the same story

Purpose

•   To increase students' knowledge and understanding of people who have significantly changed the course of history (H, CE)

•   To encourage an understanding of autobiography and biography as genres (E)

•   To help students examine how one person's work can be described from different perspectives (E, CE)

Preparation

You will need:

•   an extract from Mandela's autobiography 'The Long Walk Home' (1994, Abacus) describing his childhood: (page 11–12 is excellent, as it provides a picture of Mandela as a young boy in the countryside, learning the importance of defeating opponents without dishonouring them).

•   an extract from a current biography for children about his political struggle (e.g. in Wayland's 'Mandela' 1995, p. 16, where his defiance of authority is described).

•   a printout on Mandela from the website: Who's Who of Southern Africa: (www.news24.co.za./News24/WhosWho/0,1532,2–254,00). This gives a brief account of the events of his life and posts held: it contains many facts and dates.

Procedure

With the whole class, establish who has heard of Mandela and of South Africa. Explain the key features of apartheid, with a globe to hand to show the location of South Africa. If possible have a video clip or photographs of Mandela to show the class. Explain how democracy is developing in South Africa and that international pressure groups are assisting that process.

Establish that they are going to learn something about the life of this person from three sources: his own account, the account of a biographer, and an account from a 'factual compendium'. Might these three accounts be different? In what ways? Elicit the main features of biography and autobiography – have two columns on the board. Now divide the students into groups of three and give each group one of the three texts. In their groups, students must read the text and write brief notes on what they have learnt about Mandela from their reading. They then report this back. Compile a list of key points of Mandela's life and indicate the sources (e.g. autobiography, biography or Who's Who).

Plenary

- What was Mandela's life like as a child?

- What were the key dates in his life?

- Which text gave us the most factual information?

- Which text gave us an idea of Mandela as a person?

- What are the advantages of biography, as opposed to autobiography?

- What has Mandela done to make the world a better place?

- How could we find out more about the current situation in South Africa?

Possibilities

A group can be set the task of interviewing Mandela: they must decide the ten most important questions they would like to ask him. The list could be given to another group to find some of the answers – either by reading the Wayland biography, by looking on the internet or by researching video and newspaper articles.

Work could be extended to look at the denial of rights to blacks under apartheid. Using the Wayland biography, students could list the rights Mandela was denied, giving evidence from the text. The UDHR (Universal Declaration of Human Rights) can be used as a reference (see Chapter 5). It is also important to look at the changes in South Africa since the end of apartheid, so that the focus is on progress.

Students could also study the lives of others who have fought for justice or worked with those less fortunate. Heinemann's *Profile* series includes *Nelson Mandela* and *Mother Teresa*, and Evans' *Tell Me About* series includes *Mary Seacole, Sojourner Truth, Martin Luther King* and *Emmeline Pankhurst*. There are obvious links with the history curriculum here and one would hope that if such people are studied in the English curriculum, they are also studied in history. The people in question need to be placed in their historical contexts and to be seen as part of change at that time.

Adapted from an idea from Petra Hodgson,
PGCE student, University of Exeter.

Using stories from other countries, with original texts

Purpose

- To enjoy the contribution of children's literature from other countries (CE, E)
- To raise the interest of children in other languages and cultures (G, MFL, CE)
- To make connections and comparisons between texts from different cultures (E).

Preparation

You will need a story from another county in translation, and if possible the text in the original language (see Resources section). It is preferable that this lesson is part of a series of lessons familiarising children with the chosen country. Use an OHT or have an enlarged photocopy of a page of original text with some easily identifiable words. You may like to 'get in the mood' by handing round a small snack peculiar to the country in question, e.g. tortillas.

Procedure

Explain to the children that they are going to be looking at a text from another country and ask them to look at the original text page in front of them. Keep the translation hidden. Ask the children if they can guess what some of the words might mean. Show them the cover of the book and any illustrations and from all these clues ask them to predict what they think the story might be about. (An alternative to this would be to have given one group the original text to study beforehand, so that they are ready with ideas.)

Produce the English version and first of all read the selected page that you have on the OHT, in translation, asking the children to watch out for their own word guesses. Discuss how close they are and introduce the idea of the influences of other languages and therefore cultures, on English. Read the rest of an appropriate section of the book in English. Predict the ending of the story. Put the children in groups and ask them to research the influence of the particular language on English and collect examples. Then ask them to write a paragraph from the point of view of a character/characters in the section read.

Plenary

- What have you learnt about the influence of this language on English?
- What clues are there to the way people live in the country of your book?
- What similarities and differences are there between children's lives in that country and ours?
- What more would you like to find out?

Possibilities

You could widen the links to more than just one lesson, making it part of a project on, for example, Europe. Other literacy links could include using myths/legends from the country concerned, e.g. 'The Shawl' is a Spanish folk tale with useful Spanish words included in an English text. You could focus on layout of books, find title, author, publisher, blurb. Is the layout the same? Extend the work through visiting linguists or people who are familiar with the culture of your chosen country. Children could learn to speak some of the language, perhaps learn a small play/song to perform in assembly. They could also prepare/eat food.

Case study

A small village primary school with two classes took part in a European Comenius project 'Only Connect' which used translations of children's literature alongside the original texts to promote greater understanding amongst European children. They used a French book *Dutch Without Tears*, a Spanish book *What a Terrible Child!* and a Greek story *City of the Deep*.

The teacher of the top class (Years 4, 5 and 6) extended the literacy hour and linked the work with the humanities and music and art. She felt that the children had 'enjoyed the stories which had nice twists in them' and was particularly surprised at the enthusiasm of the lower ability children who 'were really into investigating texts in other languages. Perhaps this was because it was a level playing field for them they could have a stab at words'. She invited in a local French speaker and cooked Spanish food. She felt it was important to use the translation 'alongside the original because then that language is the connection: you can look at the similarities and the differences between the two'. The focus of the project was on books from Europe and the teacher commented:

> I don't think I would have thought about this before the project. I had always thought of cross-cultural links as remote but actually it's these near links that are important. Particularly the European ones and this business of being European.

The children were able to see the connections between their own lives and those of the children in the stories:

> I think I'm a bit like the boy because I'm always losing things.

> In Dutch Without Tears, he's a bit like my sister because she likes languages.

They also commented on the process of looking at texts in the original language, which they thought were 'fun because you can guess words and find out what they really are'. One concluded: 'Stories are the same. Children are children and we like stories whatever country they come from'.

With thanks to Anne Jones and Years 4 and 5,
Christow School.

Language never stands still

Purpose

- To help students appreciate that English as a language is constantly evolving (CE, E)
- To encourage students to appreciate the many different forms of English (CE, E)
- To provide opportunities for speculation about the future of English (CE)

Preparation

You will need copies of 'Language never stands still' (Handout 8) for each pair of students.

Procedure

Give one copy of Handout 8 to each pair of students. They can work on one or more of the following:

Extract A: extracts from the 1663 and 1976 versions of the bible: the parable of the lost son (Luke 15v.14–16).
In your pairs, work out how many years separate these two translations of the bible. Which version of the extract is easier to understand? Why? Which words do you not understand?

Extract B: old words/new words. The 'old words' are ones we rarely use today.
In your pairs match the words from the 'old words' list with those from the 'new words' list. Which words do you not understand? What 'old words' do you recognise? Are any of these used by your parents or grandparents? Why do you think the words have changed?

Extract C: new words in the dictionary.
Some publishers of dictionaries have tried to find one special word which was used for the first time in a particular year. This list shows some from the Collins dictionary. In your pairs choose three and think about what it tells you about this word. Which word would you choose for this year? For next year?

Extract D: English overseas.
English is spoken in the U.S.A., but some words are different or mean something different. In pairs, match up the words that mean the same thing. What other words from other English speaking countries do you know that are different? Why do you think this might be?

Plenary

Discuss each activity in turn, clarifying the meaning of any difficult words.

- Which words were hardest to work out? Why?
- Why do you think English has changed?
- Could we stop the language changing? Would we want to?
- Why do they use different words in the U.S.A.? (some are older versions of U.K. words which travelled to the U.S.A. in the seventeenth century, e.g. 'fall', others are words for new things).
- What other countries use different forms of English?
- How might language change in the future?

Possibilities

Students could go on to do 'The Word House Game' where they look at the contribution of many languages to English. This can be found in *Local Citizen: Global Citizen* (Christian Aid). They can also look at the variety of English within the U.K. and can study in more depth the dialect and vocabulary of other English speaking countries (eg 'sprying' for 'raining very lightly', and 'jook' for 'jab' or 'poke', in the Caribbean).

With thanks to Margot Brown (Centre for Global Education, York) and Di Durie (South Yorks DEC).

LANGUAGE NEVER STANDS STILL

ENGLISH OVER TIME

A

And when he had spent all, there arose a mighty famine in that land and he began to be in want. And he went and joined himself to a citizen of that country; and he sent him into his fields to feed swine. And he fain would have filled his belly with the husks the swine did eat; and no man gave unto him.

The Authorised Version of the Bible, 1663

A

He spent everything he had. Then a severe famine spread over that country, and he was left without a thing. So he went to work for one of the citizens of that country, who sent him out to his farm to take care of the pigs. He wished he could fill himself with the bean pods the pigs ate, but no one gave him anything to eat.

The Good News Bible, 1976

B

Old Words

muffler, wireless, peeler, needle, gramophone, parlour, distemper, (or whitewash), costume, rouge, charabang, chesterfield, attaché case, perambulator, gaberdine, locomotive, warming pan, jerry, slacks, continental quilt, jumper

B

New Words

emulsion paint, duvet, suit (women's), raincoat, police officer, sweater, stylus, blusher, scarf, disc player, settee, potty, car, hot water bottle, coach, pram, brief case, sitting room, trousers (women's), radio

C

1897 : Aspirin	1920 : Robot
1901 : Fingerprint	1926 : Television
1902 : Teddy Bear	1936 : Mickey Mouse
1907 : Allergy	1938 : Nylon

1947 : Flying saucer	
1951 : Discothèque	
1956 : Lego	
1986 : Mexican wave	
1994 : World Wide Web	

ENGLISH OVERSEAS

D

America	U.K.
trunk	flat
preserve	curtains
diaper	pavement
yard	baby's dummy
ladybug	boot
drapes	bumper
apartment	petrol
pants	rubbish
sidewalk	semi-detached house
subway	biscuit
fender	pig
elevator	tights
muffler	maize
pantihose	garden
hog	underground
corn	ladybird
gasoline	car
garbage	silencer
cookie	nappy
duplex	jam
automobile	trousers
pacifier	lift
fall	autumn

Using poetry to discuss issues of identity, language and loss, and for text level work

Purpose

- To increase students' understanding of the complex nature of identity (CE)
- To foster an understanding of poetry as a powerful vehicle for discussing the impact of grief and separation (E, CE, PSHE)
- To increase students' understanding of the economy of poetic language by paying special attention to telling details (E)

Preparation

You will need:

- an OHT of the poem 'Grandpapa'
- a copy of the poem 'Grandpapa' for each child
- sets of three differently coloured pens for students to annotate the poems
- a glossary of the French words used in the poem

Procedure

Whole class

Begin with asking questions about the idea of coming from a 'mixed' background.

- What do we mean by that?
- Do we only mean 'mixed race', or are there other ways in which a child or family can be said to be of 'mixed' heritage?
- What if both parents the same racially but are from different nationalities?
- What would it feel like to have family – grandparents, uncles and aunts, cousins – whom you found it difficult to talk to or get to know very well because, although you were related to them, you didn't live in their country or see them often?
- How would you feel when one of them died? Would it be the same as if a relation from the country you lived in died?
- And what would that tell you about where you were from yourself?

Explain that they are going to look at a poem which raises some of these issues. Read the poem on the OHT asking for immediate responses to it. Hand out copies of the poem and sets of coloured pens.

Group work

Put the students in groups of three. Each group must read the poem once. Explain that they are to use the coloured pens to annotate the poems: first colour to mark descriptions of Grandpapa; second colour to mark lines/phrases which indicate to the reader a sense of separation between the speaker of the poem and Grandpapa; third colour to mark lines/phrases which are concerned with language and language differences. As the groups report back, scribe a list of their comments.

Plenary

- Pull together comments from the groups, emphasising the importance of language reinforcing our sense of identity and belonging.

- Discuss with the class the sense of ambiguity in the poem: is it a poem of out and out grief, or is it asking questions about the nature of grief? Can you feel loss for someone you did not know well?

- Draw out examples from the groups where more than one colour was used to annotate a particular line or phrase. What does this tell us about the economy of poetic language? What does this tell us about writing which deals with complex personal issues?

Possibilities

Students can write a poem in response to their work on 'Grandpapa' which involves writing to a relation of theirs using the title 'What I'd like to say to you'. The writing may be about shared memories, conversations, rules, childhood, clothes, anything. They should write freely (5 minutes max.) in response to that title. They must keep their hands moving across the page. They must tell the truth. When they get stuck, they write the title out again as a prompt. From this free writing students are to quarry at least four lines or phrases, the ones they are most pleased with, to make a new poem. The new poem can keep the same title, or a new title may suggest itself while they are writing it.

Possibilities plus

Three other poems to look at which deal in an honest way with the death of relations are William Carlos Williams' 'The Last Words of my English Grandmother' (*The Poetry Book*, Fiona Waters (ed.), Dolphin, 1998); Norman Macaig's 'Aunt Julia' (*The Poetry Book for Primary Schools*, Anthony Wilson with Siân Hughes (eds.), Poetry Society, 1998); and Theodore Roethke's 'Elegy' (*Poetry in the Making*, Ted Hughes, Faber, 1967). Poems which deal with identity and relatives are 'English cousin comes to Scotland' by Jackie Kay (from '*Two's Company*' Puffin, 1994) and 'Bubah and Zaida' by Michael Rosen (from '*Quick, Let's Get Out of Here*', Puffin, 1985).

With thanks to Anthony Wilson, poet and tutor,
University of Exeter.

Grandpapa

Marcel Robert, 1899–1977

You were plum tree blossom and mothball smells,
black braces on a white shirt, and anger

that might at any moment explode
into the utmost care.

You tended your garden
with your watchmaker's precision,

fighting all your life with your heart,
the ticker you couldn't rely on.

Your only word of English was *Goodbye*
followed by a laugh rasping on itself

blunting the joke we couldn't see.
To greet us you pinched our cheeks

as if squeezing us into speech
then your hard, just-shaved kiss

which sighed as your head bent near us.
We learned *Bonjour, Merci, S'il-te-plait?*,

Bonne nuit and *Dors bien*; to break our bread
with our hands, and to sip black tea.

It was on your last holiday with us when we talked,
a hot Cornish fortnight where you ordered cream

every day. Our tongues unmoored themselves
the time we fished for mackerel,

you, a mountain-man and us,
wide-eyed from the suburbs.

You still caught the most,
as you shrugged with that wheezy laugh,

delighted to ride your luck,
a perfectionist visited by chance.

It was gravy, all of it – your grandchildren
growing; sea breezes spooning the air you craved;

and your straw hat sunning itself,
bleaching to its small obstinate rim.

Anthony Wilson

Acknowledgement: *How Far From Here Is Home?* (Stride, 1996)

Tackling prejudice through literature

(This activity could be done as a single lesson using the extract, but it would be highly desirable to do it in the context of reading the whole text.)

Purpose

- To think about cultural issues and their sources (E,CE)
- To use the imagination to consider other people's experiences (E,CE)
- To understand how familiar themes are explored in different cultural contexts (E, CE)
- To identify the perspectives offered on individuals, community and society (E, CE)

Preparation

You will need:

- an extract from Anita Desai's *A Village by the Sea* describing the festival of Diwali.
- a gridsheet for paired discussion with two columns headed 'Diwali' and 'Bonfire Night' and 'Similarities' written in a large font across the top of the sheet.

Procedure

Begin by doing a 'guided meditation' on memories of Bonfire Night – ask students to close their eyes and think about their recollections of Bonfire Night. Use questions to prompt their mental visualisation e.g. What colours do you see? What do people's faces look like? What do the fireworks smell like? How warm or cold do you feel? Can you smell or taste any food? Individually, students jot down words and images they associate with Bonfire Night. Read the Diwali extract from *A Village by the Sea*. In pairs, students complete the gridsheet, using their reading of the extract and their own memories of Bonfire Night to list the ways in which the two celebrations are similar. If necessary, support younger or less able students by asking them to write the key elements of Diwali in one column and then encouraging them to think about the parallels on Bonfire Night.

Plenary

- Class discussion: draw together findings, helping students to see that initial differences have deeper similarities.
- Invite students to note any important differences between Diwali and Bonfire Night.

Possibilities

Ask students to write in role as a Hindu child describing his/her memories of Diwali, conveying the excitement and atmosphere of the event. Use the text as a basis for details. Pursue the idea of superficial cultural differences masking deeper similarities: eg weddings and festivals

With thanks to Debra Myhill, University of Exeter.

4

Community into School

A person is a person through other persons. I am because you are. (Makhudu, talking about the concept of Ubuntu 1993)

Neither human existence nor individual liberty can be sustained for long outside the interdependent and over-lapping communities to which we all belong. Nor can any community long survive unless its members dedicate some of their attention, energy and resources to shared projects. (Etzioni 1997)

I want more bins, more hospitals, more hostels. Less traffic. I'm worried that there will be more violence, robbery and unemployment. (Children talking about their local area: Hicks and Holden, 1995)

Introduction

It is perhaps strange that schools are uncertain how to teach about community and community involvement when they themselves are institutional represent-ations of 'the community'. Perhaps it is because teachers are aware of potential differences and tensions in the community that they are hesitant about making these links. In spite of this, schools have a continuing concern to provide a curriculum that is relevant to children's lives. A part of this means providing opportunities for students to learn how to become 'helpfully involved in the life and concerns of their neighbourhood and communities, including learning through community involvement and service' (QCA 2000: 5).

Key issues

Sense of community

How can children develop an understanding of the different communities to which they belong? How can they begin to appreciate and become respectful of difference? How can they develop a sense of the interdependence between different groups? How can we develop schools so that they become a resource for the communities that they serve?

Community involvement

How can teachers identify community members who have relevant knowledge and expertise to support children's learning? How can teachers and children identify issues in the community for research and action? How can the global dimensions of the local community be understood? How can the interests of minority groups be represented?

The status of learning through involvement
in the community

How will learning through involvement in the community enhance the curriculum? What is the relationship between this new knowledge and the prescribed curriculum? How can this work be assessed and evaluated? How can children's involvement with the community become a means for learning about the processes of democratic change?

Recent research findings

Sense of community

The term 'community' is much used, and yet understood in many different ways. Current sociological perspectives stress that definitions of community remain contested. There is a growing consensus that community is not bound by spatial/locational boundaries especially given the development of information communication technologies (Castells 1991). At the same time the power of imaginary dimensions of community has been recognised (Anderson 1991), making the process of linking experience of community to the development of personal and social identity the more difficult. For example, Hoggett's research of the Bangladeshi community in London's East End points to significant changes. Whilst the Bangladeshi community has shifted from a primary identification with secular nationalism to an embrace of Islam, within this overall shift a whole number of other identities have emerged for radicalised young Bangladeshi women and street-wise young males (Hoggett 1997).

Community involvement

At the same time concern has been expressed about the lack of interest in and involvement of young people in public and political life. Research findings summarised in the *Final Report of the Advisory Group on Citizenship* (QCA 1998) indicate a continuing 'political disconnection' of young people (Wilkinson and Muglan 1995; Jowell and Park 1997). The QCA report draws attention to the submission from the British Youth Council which emphasises the significance of 'democracy' and 'community' to the processes of citizenship education. Education should 'help them to see where and how they fit into the community. It should help them to understand their community, its history, what part it has played in national life'.

The Policy Studies Institute argues in its report *Ethnic Minorities in Britain: Diversity and Disadvantage* (1997) that an explicit idea of multicultural citizenship needs to be formulated in Britain. A more plural approach to racial disadvantage requires forms of citizenship which are sensitive to ethnic diversity and offer respect to individuals and the social groups to which they feel they belong. These sentiments have been echoed in the recent report, *The Future of Multi-Ethnic Britain*, where the authors argue that 'Britain is both a community of citizens and a community of communities, both a liberal and a multi-cultural society, [with] sometimes conflicting requirements' (Runnymede 2000: ix).

The status of learning through involvement in the community

An important source for the educational principle of community action and involvement is the work of the OECD/ENSI (Environment and School Initiatives) programme as reported by Elliott (1998) and Posch and Mair (1997). The ENSI project included sustained attempts to provide students with opportunities to research problems within their own environments and communities and to use the new knowledge gained as a basis for interaction, learning and action in the locality. Environmental education was the pretext for exploring community relationships, civic literacy, the nature of democracy and the implications of citizenship. The outcomes of this project reflect what Hargreaves (1982) calls the community-centred curriculum and is consistent with Bentley's more recently formulated notion of schools as 'neighbourhood learning centres' (Bentley 1998: 186).

Research conducted by Hicks and Holden with children aged 7–18 indicates that they are interested in working for change and that many are involved in taking action in the community either as individuals or as part of organisations outside the school context. 'They feel responsible as citizens of the future for what may happen, but lack a clear vision of what their own part in this might be' (Hicks and Holden 1995:112). Education for citizenship can provide a framework and a focus for these concerns.

Activities

Myself in the community

Purpose

- To give children a sense of the range of groups/communities to which different members of the class belong (CE)
- To support children in understanding why people join different groups (CE)
- To support children in becoming respectful of differences between groups/communities (CE)

Preparation

Provide pictures that give information about groups/communities that children and young people belong to. These might include membership of a youth club, a religious community, a football supporters' club, an art/dance group, outdoor adventure groups.

Procedure

Use the pictures to stimulate a whole class discussion about the kinds of groups which young people belong to. Identify groups to which the children belong and list these on a board or flipchart.

Group work

In small groups, ask the children to

- identify three groups to which anybody from this class could belong

- identify three which only certain people can belong to

- identify the purposes of the different groups identified

Plenary

Each group should report back to the rest of the class.

- What purposes did the groups have in common?

- Why are some groups exclusive in their membership? Is this right?

- What are the benefits of belonging to a group?

- How could we encourage others to join a group?

Possibilities

Ask each child to design a badge which illustrates the different groups/communities of which they are members and which represents herself/himself in the community.

Learning about the work of community groups

Purpose

- To provide information about community groups in the locality (CE, G)

- To help students understand how community groups function – and whether they do paid or voluntary work (CE)

- To help students understand how community groups make a difference to other peoples' lives (CE, PSHE)

Preparation

Provide information (pictures, leaflets, summary accounts) of the work and membership of different groups which work in and for the community. These may include environmental groups, a playgroup, drama group, a community care group, neighbourhood watch group. Details of groups like these are obtainable from the local library, local council or local community centre.

Procedure

As a whole class, discuss the meaning of the term 'community group' and agree a provisional definition. Working in small groups, ask students to research the group for which they have written handouts and prepare a poster for display which provides the following information:

- The name of the community group

- The aim of the community group

- The way the group works

- The people who benefit from the work of the groups

Plenary

Each group should give a presentation about the community group that they have been studying. Then discuss:

- Why do people join community groups like these?

- In what ways do they make a difference to people's lives?

- Are there any other ways that this kind of work could be done?

- Are there any community groups which you think should exist and don't?

Possibilities

Students can design a poster advertising the community group of their interest, encouraging people to become an active member of the group. Invite a representative from a local community group to visit the class and talk about the work of the group.

School in the community: a living map

Purpose

- To raise self-esteem, by allowing children to identify themselves as valued members of the community (CE)

- To give children an understanding of the life of a community and how it is always changing (CE, G)

- To help children understand the use of maps, with a key (G)

Preparation

You will need:

- A1 paper (depending on the scale you want to use)

- masking tape or Blu-tac

- pens and cards of different colours

- a map of the local area

Procedure

Working with the children, select the area you want to cover, and draw a large-scale map making sure all the children's houses are marked on it. If one child lives very far away, you can always add an extra piece of paper. To do this start with a reference point (e.g. a river, school building, etc.) and then get the children to help you add social elements (houses, play-grounds, etc.), economic elements (shops, agricultural fields, etc.) and natural elements (woods, rivers, hills, etc.).

Now ask the children to decide on things that could change regularly during the year. These could include birthdays, deaths, births, pregnancies, parties, visits from friends or family. All of these will be represented by symbols. An example: Julie's mother is pregnant so next to her house we place a symbol of a big belly and when her mother gives birth, we change the symbol for a new baby symbol. In addition, ask each child to put a symbol (e.g. a star) on the map to represent a place that is special to them: this could be part of the woods or the local skate park. You will need to make the symbols small but clear. Use masking tape or Blu-tac so that they can be moved around the map during the year. Ensure your map has a place title (e.g. Dartmouth, U.K. or Oscollopata, South Peru) and that rivers and roads are named. Each house should have the name of its respective child.

Plenary (weekly)

It is important to use the map for a short period of time (15 min.) every week to keep children involved and feeling part of the community. Before moving around the symbols (and adding new ones) you could ask:

- What has changed in our community over the last week?

- What is planned for this week?

- Is there anything new you want to add?

51

Possibilities

There is scope for mathematical investigation: how many houses in streets, number of people in houses, who lives the furthest from school, etc. There are also geographical links: map work looking at different routes from x to y, and physical geography focusing on river bends, hills, etc. Linking with history, older people can come and talk about how it used to be, using the map as a reference. Children can relate to changes in the community during consecutive years, if the school administration holds on to the maps (new buildings, street changes, etc.).

With thanks to Tim De Winter.

Tim De Winter, former educational consultant for UNICEF in Peru writes:

This activity was always very popular with teachers as well as pupils because of the broad range of interactions that were possible. During the time I worked in Peru, this activity was used successfully in schools and I also used it for my enquiries about school-aged children who didn't participate at school, to find out how long they walked before getting to school on an empty stomach, and so on.

My town, my future

Purpose

- To plan a community for the future, based on current concerns (G, CE)

- To consider the physical and social needs of a community (G, CE, RE)

- To develop map-making skills (G)

- To help students understand the role of the law in protecting communities (CE)

Preparation

You will need a large sheet of sugar paper or other A1 paper for each group and felt-tip pens.

Procedure

Start the class thinking about what makes a good town and what facilities are needed in relation to their own town or city:

What do we like about our town (city)?

What would we choose to show visitors?

Which areas need improving?

What is currently being planned for our town?

What do we need here that we don't have?

Explain to the class that even now architects and town planners are making decisions that will affect their town (or village or city) in a few years time. Towns do not just change: people make decisions about how they will change according to priorities, costs, etc. Local and national governments are also busy making decisions about laws and regulations, which will affect people's way of life. For the purpose of this activity, students are to have the chance to plan a new town for 20 years hence, or they can remodel their existing town. Money is not an issue though they will have to justify its use. Environmental issues must be considered.

Questions to consider:

- What facilities do young people need in a town or city?

- What do the elderly need?

- What about newcomers?

- What about people with physical disabilities?

- What about the homeless?

- What about the needs of other groups (e.g. families)?

In addition to considering the needs of different groups, you can ask students to think about the transport system they want, meeting places, places of worship, schools etc. After they have drawn the plans for their town, ask each group to agree on what laws they want in their community in order to protect people's rights and have the town function effectively. They can also consider what punishments or sanctions there would be for those who break these laws. When all groups have completed their towns and laws, pin them on the walls for all to look at. See p. 54 for an example.

Plenary

- How have you taken into account the needs of different groups?

- Were there any problems meeting these various needs?

- How were environmental and sustainability issues considered?

- Would you like to live in these towns? Why?

- What rules or rights did people have?

- How were these enforced?

- How different are these to current laws?

Possibilities

This activity can be made more complex by giving each group a particular brief – e.g. design a town with the needs of children in mind, or the needs of elderly people. The groups can then compare their various plans and discuss where the conflicts lie and how these might be resolved. This activity can also lead to action in the real world. Students can study their own locality, looking at changes currently being planned or changes they would like to see happen. They can invite in local councillors, town planners or community group leaders to discuss how changes might be brought about.

53

Rules for our town:

Everyone is allowed to go skateboarding or rollerblading in the park but it is your responsibility if you get hurt.

Everyone can use the church, synagogue or mosque.

Everyone must keep to the rules. These are:

- use bikes when you can
- pick up all your litter
- look after our river (no pollution)
- keep in the speed limit and wear seat belts
- don't smoke
- don't pull down old houses

N.B. There is a fine of 500 euros if you break the rules.

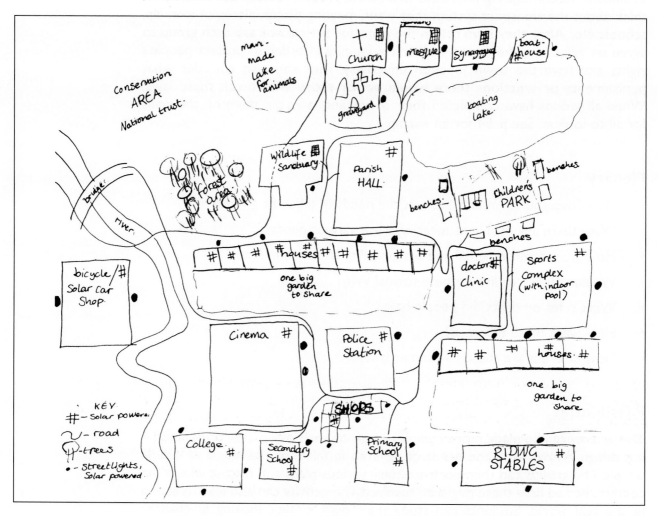

Our town in the future (Year 6, Sandford School).

Investigating the world of work in the community

Purpose

- To help students understand that there are many different kinds of work undertaken in the community (CE)

- To help students evaluate the different contributions of people in the community (CE)

Preparation

Copy the set of pictures (Handout 10) so that you have one set for each pair of students.

Procedure

You might want to start with a brief brainstorm about what jobs the class thinks exist in the community and which they think is most important, to model the process. Then give out one set of pictures to each pair. Ask them to rank the pictures in diamond formation, i.e.:

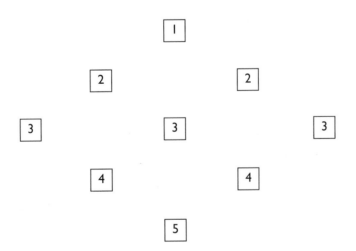

using the criteria of 'most important to the community'. The picture of the worker who is considered most important to the community is placed at the top of the diamond, then the next two are equal second. The three across the centre are next equal and so on. The one at the foot is considered least important. When the pairs have completed their task they form into groups of six and each pair explains and seeks to justify its ranking to the other two pairs. The six then negotiate a consensus ranking for the whole group.

Plenary

- Which work was considered the most important by each group? Why?

- Which was considered the least important? Why?

- What influenced your decisions?

- What do you think the actual people would say about their work?

- What jobs have been left out that you think should have been included?

- What jobs would you like to find out more about?

Possibilities

This activity could be repeated but with the criteria 'Who do you think gets paid the most?' Discussion could then follow about whether both rankings were the same. If not, why not? What should be the main influences on how people are paid? Are there any issues raised with regard to equal opportunities? An alternative opening to this activity is to give the children a picture each (of the community members) and ask them to write three sentences about why this person is valued.

Adapted from an activity by Pam Pointon,
University of Cambridge.

Possibilities for older students

Students can be asked to collect information about chosen workplaces in the community. Arrangements would need to be made for small groups of students to make a visit, observe employees at work and conduct focused interviews to collect data to inform discussion about issues such as:

- The variety of work opportunities in the local community

- The needs of local employers

- Employment practices in relation to equal opportunities

- Opportunities for young people from the local communities

- Employers' response to environmental issues with specific reference to Local Agenda 21 (use of energy, recycling, control of waste).

Then and now: 150 years of change in the community

Purpose

- To help students understand that communities are always changing (H, G, CE)
- To help students value the voice of the elderly (H, CE)
- To allow for some negotiation of the curriculum (CE)
- To look forwards as well as backwards (H, CE)

Preparation

You will need some of the following:

Local census material (illustrating who lived where and employment practices), school records, family artefacts, access to elderly people who have lived in the community for a long time, adults prepared to take groups of students out to look at local buildings or interview people, resource books on the history of the local area, old newspapers and photographs.

Procedure

Explain to the students that they are going to be able to choose an aspect of the history of their local area to study. Start the discussion by asking:

A hundred years ago ...

- What jobs did people do here?
- Who lived here?
- What buildings were here? What did houses look like?
- What was our school like?
- What artefacts did people have in their homes?
- What kind of transport did people use?
- What kinds of clothes did they wear?

Students then divide into groups and decide if there is one of the above they would like to research or if there is an area which has not been mentioned yet. Provide the resources available and encourage as many groups as possible to go into the local area as part of their research (e.g. to look at old buildings, to visit the public records office, to interview elderly people). Each group should produce a time line which shows the history of their particular aspect 150 years ago, 100 years ago, 50 years ago and then at the present time.

Plenary

•   What things have changed the most?

•   What caused change?

•   What did you learn from interviewing elderly people that surprised you?

•   Is every new thing better? Why or why not?

•   Would you have liked to live in this community 100 years ago?

•   How do you think children in 100 years will view us?

•   What might we choose to leave as artefacts and evidence?

Possibilities

Students could extend their time lines to look to the future. Thus a group looking at housing could plan a house for 2050, a group looking at transport could think about current traffic problems and plan for local transport for 50 years hence, etc.

Causes and consequences: people on the move

Purpose

- To help students understand that people have always moved from place to place (H, CE)

- To show that there are many different reasons for people moving (H, G, CE)

- To illustrate how their own community, like all communities, is constantly changing (G, CE)

- To recognise the rights of newcomers and the responsibilities of the host community (CE)

Preparation

You will need information about some of the principle migrations to the local area in the last 100 years, and the reasons for this movement.

Procedure

In pairs, students discuss who in their immediate family has moved (e.g. parents, grandparents, aunts) and then whether any close friends have moved. They select three or four examples and record the reasons for these movements. (This might involve some research at home.) Then call the class together and put five headings on the board:

- economic (moving for a better job or promotion)

- social (to be near family and friends)

- environmental (to be in a different kind of environment, e.g. countryside or city)

- political (to escape war and persecution)

- other

Ask the students for examples (from their work in pairs) to go under each heading. Discussion points:

- what are the main reasons for people moving?

- what methods of transport did they use?

- what would have happened to these people if they had not been allowed to move?

- how would our community have been different?

- what do you think these people felt like when they first moved?

- how might people have helped them?

Then provide information about some of the principal migrations to the local area in the last 100 years, and the reasons for this movement. You also need information on groups currently arriving in the local area and information about who is working to help these groups. After further discussion in small groups draw the class together.

Plenary

- What people are moving into this community now?

- What difficulties may they face?

- What could we learn from them?

- How could we help them as individuals and as a school?

Possibilities

This work could also be linked with the Key Stage 2 History Study Unit, Britain since 1930s, and a local history study. Students could interview elderly citizens (witnesses to change) and those whose families have moved into the community more recently. Another possibility is to use the activity to lead into work looking at the quality of life for the different groups of the community. Interviews can provide a way in.

Before interviewing people, students need to consider how to be sensitive in the questions they ask. This guidance may help:

Field work interview questions: preparation

- Before you begin to ask a question always ask yourself, would I be happy to answer this question?

- Remember you are trying to get the people you are interviewing to tell you about their lives so they must feel they can trust you.

- You must guarantee that you will not pass on the information you have got to anyone other than the student group you will work with.

- You may find it easier to talk to groups of people rather than individuals.

Interviewing members of the community: some ideas

- What are the things you like about living in this community?

- Do you feel comfortable living in this community?

- Do you have any problems living in this community? What are they?

- Do you think that the national and local governments understand your problems?

- What would make your life in this community easier?

- What do you remember about going to school? Is it different for your children or the children in your community?

- How many languages do you speak? What language do you usually sing and dance in?

5

Extending Social and Moral Education

Circle time is to learn to be friendly, to listen, to stop arguing, to make you work together no matter what. (Boy, aged 8)

If I have the right to play, I must let the others play with my things as well and so we become friends playing. (Girl, aged 7, San Sebastian-Cusco, Peru)

Violence is going up – it's because teenagers don't get the understanding they need – you see it on TV – crime's going up, the suicide rate's up. (Boy, aged 14)

Introduction

All schools would claim to teach social and moral education in some form, as teachers recognise that good social skills, including co-operation and respect, are fundamental to effective teaching and learning. Likewise a sense of what is right and wrong is taught from the early years and will be fostered throughout a child's school career, whether in collective worship, through class discussions on moral issues or through the use of sanctions and rewards. However, to meet the requirements of education for citizenship, social and moral education must go beyond teaching right and wrong and good behaviour. Teachers will need to build on current practice in PSHE (personal, social and health education) to ensure that ethical issues beyond the school are addressed and that young people are helped to develop a values framework which will inform their judgement and actions. These values would relate to the virtues identified in the National Curriculum – truth, justice, honesty, trust and sense of duty, as discussed in Chapter 1.

Key issues

Self-esteem and identity

How can we ensure that through social and moral education, children acquire a positive self-image? How we help them to value their own work, their own identity and their own cultural background? How can we encourage children to be tolerant and understanding of others?

Respecting the voice of the child

How can we ensure that the social and moral issues we raise as teachers for discussion are those most relevant to children's lives? How can we enable even the most timid children to voice their opinions? How can we create a classroom ethos where children are listened to and respected?

Acquiring a values system

How can we foster in each child values which are based on truth, justice, honesty, trust and sense of duty? How can we teach human rights as a value system? What is the place of religious values in schools? How do we deal with children who express a values system which is different from our own? How do we encourage values-based participation?

Recent research findings

Self-esteem and identity

There is increasing recognition that effective teaching must concern itself with children's social and moral education. This includes the fostering of social skills, good interpersonal relationships, empathetic judgement, person perception, and moral judgement. (Meisels *et al.* 1995). Such skills are fundamental to the formation of identity, that is the way children see themselves, how they see others and how they in turn are seen by others. One of the aims of effective teaching must be to foster positive self-identity and students' self-esteem. Indeed, Pollard and Filer argue that it is only when their self-esteem and self-confidence is high that children become effective learners. 'The need for suitable social conditions in classrooms complements the necessity for appropriate levels of cognitive challenge' (1996: 317). Bruner goes further; for him 'a failure to equip minds with the skills for understanding and feeling and acting in the cultural world is not simply scoring a pedagogical zero. It risks creating alienation, defiance and practical incompetence' (1996: 43). With regard to citizenship education, then, effective social and moral education must provide students with the confidence to be able to voice their opinions, to listen to others, to empathise, and to make moral judgements. They must know that their opinions are of value and that they are valued as people.

Respecting the voice of the child

In western societies, a belief in childhood innocence and a concern to protect children from the responsibilities of adulthood, has led to the creation of a 'cosy curriculum' in some primary schools (Wood, 1998). And yet we know that children as young as seven have concerns about the environment, are developing views on poverty and injustice and are aware of global issues (Hicks and Holden, 1995). Children need a forum for discussing their hopes and fears and for raising questions; they need to discuss social and moral issues both inside and outside the school. In many primary schools, circle time is one such forum, where the use of a 'magic microphone' ensures that all take turns and are listened to. But teachers need to ensure that they do not always set the agenda or use circle time to sort out behaviour problems. Opportunities need to be provided for children to raise their own concerns and take the initiative.

The issues in secondary school are perhaps even more pertinent where pressure on the curriculum means that PSHE is often covered in tutorial time. Rudduck *et al.* maintain that the secondary curriculum and school environment do not reflect the social maturity of students today and are 'founded upon an outdated view of childhood which fails to acknowledge children's capacity to reflect on issues affecting their lives' (Rudduck1995: 172). Griffith also warns of the danger of curriculum content unrelated to experiences or interests of the pupils and to the wider social world thus 'existing without external relevance' (Griffith 1996: 209). The challenge for teachers is to listen to students' concerns and interests and facilitate genuine debate. This debate, however, must be informed so that ignorance does not debate with ignorance, and thus the teacher's role is one of provider of information and promoter of authentic discussion.

Acquiring a values system

> Circle time is not necessarily citizenship education . . .[Such activities] don't necessarily advance children's understanding of social issues or rights or social rules or conventions. In citizenship education we are making moral conventions explicit. (Klein in TES 1998)

Klein (above) makes the point that while circle time can be an excellent forum for discussion, citizenship education requires more than this. If we are to encourage young people to voice their own opinions, we must at the same time give them the basis for forming their own independent judgements. Moral decisions are made with reference to a moral code and schools have a responsibility to develop children's value systems. Starkey (1992) maintains that any programme to promote values education is essentially concerned with human rights as these are 'internationally validated moral standards, universally accepted in principle in international discourse, even if they are not always enacted by governments' (p. 186). Human rights, he says, provide an ethical and moral framework for living in the community, whether this be local or global. Both the Universal Declaration of Human Rights (1948) and the United Nations Declaration of the Rights of the Child (1959) can be used by teachers to help students understand the importance of an individual's self-worth and dignity, equality of rights and responsibility for ensuring that the rights of others are protected. Such a universal charter is useful in schools where linguistic, cultural, religious and ethnic pluralism is now the norm.

Teaching values is a cross-curricular approach, but some parts of the curriculum may be more specifically associated with values than others, e.g. religious education where reflection and sharing are central. Good religious education does not indoctrinate because it increases student choice. It commends different world views, life stances and religions as worthy of serious study and consideration and as significant value-shaping factors in the lives of women and men over millennia. Thus human rights education and religious education both have important roles to play in education for citizenship.

Activities

Circle time

There are numerous possibilities for circle time but certain fundamental principles are common to all sessions. You should ensure that you:

- have a planned focus for the session, either as part of a progressive thematic approach, or one responsive to the class's current needs

- consider any 'key vocabulary' to support and extend the children's talk and understanding

- prepare the space with the children

- hold debriefing discussions (or plenaries) after games and activities

- are aware that activities, rounds and games can be verbal; non-verbal or physical; or art- or music-based (thus supporting children with a variety of preferred learning modes)

- establish ground rules for circle time together with the children

Some possibilities are:

- themes related to personal, social and moral education: 'getting to know you', feelings, caring and being kind, co-operation, conflict resolution, achieving, listening and concentrating, affirmation, friendship, solving problems, gender, changes.

- themes related to topical, controversial issues: what's in the news, what's happening in our local area, what's being debated in parliament

Children can take ownership of sessions by helping to plan the content. There can be a class notice board (circular?) where post-its may be stuck detailing incidents or ideas that could be dealt with in circle time. They are also wonderfully creative at adapting games and activities: their suggestions are often better than your own. Circle time also provides a point of reference for dealing with issues relating to the class as a whole: 'do you remember when . . . what did people suggest . . . how did they feel?' Books to develop circle time are numerous: see resources section.

With thanks to Olwen Goodall, University of Exeter.

65

The great divide . . . you must decide

Purpose

- To encourage reflection on values (without having to speak) (CE, PSHE)
- To encourage confidence in voicing one's opinions in a structured situation (CE,E)
- To advance students' understanding of social and moral issues (CE, PSHE)
- To help students realise that there are usually many sides to any argument (CE)
- To encourage turn-taking and listening skills (CE, E).

Preparation

You will need:

- a classroom space cleared of desks
- a ball of string or rope
- a large ball for throwing ('power ball'). An inflatable globe is ideal
- some statements to start the activity

Procedures

Put the rope or string in a straight line down the middle of the classroom and explain that this line represents 'the great divide'. One side of it represents 'I agree' and the other side 'I disagree'. Explain that as you read out the statements students must move to stand on one side of the rope or the other, according to how strongly they feel. Thus a person very strongly disagreeing would move as far away as possible from the rope in the middle, whereas someone 'not sure' would be close to or on the line. Participants do not need to explain their choice unless they want to, in which case they put up their hand and you throw them the power ball to allow them to speak. They then throw this to the next person wishing to speak. In order to keep up the pace of the activity, just allow a few to speak about each statement.

Start with simple statements, for example:

> Red is a nicer colour than blue
>
> Dogs are better than cats
>
> It is wrong to eat other animals
>
> Children should help at home

Then move on to more controversial ones, for example:

> Children should help at home if they get paid for it
>
> University education should be free
>
> The abortion pill should be freely available
>
> Refugees should be allowed into this country

N.B. The statements you choose will obviously depend on the age of your students.

66

Plenary

- How did you feel about playing this game?
- Did having the power ball give you more confidence to speak?
- Which statements caused the most controversy?
- Were you surprised at the range of opinions?

Possibilities

You can use this activity to introduce a specific issue by relating all the statements to that particular theme. You can develop the activity by getting one side to try to persuade the other to agree with them (and thus move their position physically along the line). You can also ask students to write their own statements, taking turns to read them out. They can discuss what makes a good statement to use in an exercise like this. The statement which caused the greatest discussion can be used to illustrate how a more formal debate is staged. This statement can be taken as the motion, with a chair and speakers for and against the motion, and comments taken from the floor.

I ran this activity in the secondary schools and detention centres I visited as part of 'Up With People', a community programme for young people. As facilitators we had to have good management skills as tempers could often flare ... but challenging opinions was the point after all. Besides forcing young people to think about their own personal beliefs on bigger issues, it encouraged good use of citizenship skills such as listening, reasoning and expressing feelings.

Canadian student-teacher, University of Exeter.

(More details of Up With People community programme for young people from www.upwithpeople.org)

Tricky situations: What would I do?

Purpose

- To encourage students to articulate their views and defend them in a small group (CE, E)
- To provide a forum for the discussion of social, moral and controversial issues (CE, PSHE)
- To help develop co-operative and listening skills (CE, E).

Preparation

You will need a set of context cards for each group (use those below or if you teach younger children, write your own).

Procedures

Put students in groups of between four and six and give each group a set of cards. Instruct students that the cards are to be in a pile, face down. In turn, each student is to take a card, read it aloud and give his/her opinion on the best solution *before* the others in the group have a say. This ensures that each student has a chance to articulate his/her views and that no one person dominates the discussion. Ask the groups to identify which scenarios were the hardest to resolve. Allow at least 30 minutes for this activity. Then draw the class back together.

Plenary

- Which card gave your group the most problems? Why?
- Which was the easiest to resolve? Why?
- What helped you to resolve issues?
- Do people have different moral codes, different values?
- Is there always a right or wrong answer?

Possibilities

A group that finishes early could be asked to write their own context cards for another group to resolve. They could be asked to include any issues that have caused particular problems in the school (or class).

Card 1:

Jamal has a day off for Divali celebrations. He tells his friends that this is for a religious festival. All his classmates complain that this isn't fair. You are Jamal's best friend. How do you respond?

Card 2:

A friend's brother, Martin, has just started secondary school. In PE he is given the choice of netball, football and rounders. He chooses to play netball but the other boys chant 'You're gay! You're gay!'. You hear this in the playground and want to defend him. What do you say?

Card 3:

You see Julie take some money from the locker of a younger girl. You are frightened of Julie as she is a known bully and you don't want to be picked on. What do you do?

Card 4:

You are out of school in the lunch hour and your friend takes a lipstick without paying. When you make a comment, she admits she has shop-lifted before but says that shops are covered by insurance so it's OK. She begs you not to tell her parents. What do you do?

Card 5:

Your best friend is distraught because her boyfriend has been seen with another girl at break time. She says she can't work and wants to discuss the situation in every lesson. You want to get your work done but also want to help your friend. What do you do?

With thanks to Hilary Orr and Lisa Clark, student teachers, for the context cards.

If I have the right, I also have the duty . . .

Purpose

- To promote positive behaviour (PSHE, CE)

- To encourage reflection on rights, ethics and responsibilities (CE, PSHE)

- To help students appreciate that with rights also come duties (CE)

- To introduce a tenet fundamental to many world religions (RE).

Preparation

For younger children you will need to have done some work on needs and rights and have a list of what the children consider the rights of the child: e.g. the right to play, to go to school, to have friends, to have fun. For older students, after some discussion of what is meant by 'children's rights' you can use a copy of the *Convention on the Rights of the Child* (www.unicef.org/crc/fulltext.htm or see Resources section). Make sure that the copy of the Convention is written in accessible language.

Procedures

Write the basic principle on the blackboard:

What you do not wish done to yourself, do not do to others

Or in positive terms:

What you wish done to yourself, do to others

As a whole class discuss the meaning of this. You could link this to the Christian tenet 'Do unto others as you would have them do to you' or to similar tenets from other religions. Make sure they understand the difference between positive and negative terms (as in the two statements above). A good example is the difference between 'do not lie' and 'be honest', because the positive statement implies a lot more. Then put students into groups of three to four. Younger children can work with some of the rights they have identified earlier, older students can be asked to select a few (three to five) articles from the *Convention on the Rights of the Child*. In their groups they must copy out each right they have selected and then decide on the duty that goes with the right.

An example is:

If you have the right to life, you also have the duty not to kill.

Students can then be encouraged to write their duties in a more positive way, referring to the opening principle. The example then becomes:

If you have the right to life, you also have the duty to respect life.

The students should then come back together as a class to share their work.

70

Plenary

- What did you learn about the rights of children?

- What do you think are the most important of the duties written by each group?

- How could we help each other to be responsible and carry out these duties?

- What would happen if we demanded our rights and did not think about duties?

- What organisations are working world-wide to encourage people to act responsibly?

Possibilities

This activity can be used as a basis for making class or school rules. It encourages a positive approach towards rights and responsibilities rather than a list of rules headed 'you must not'. It also helps children find new ways to resolve problems and challenges as it encourages a positive, responsible approach.

I have the right to express myself but I should think twice before speaking because I may hurt somebody else and say something stupid I may regret later. (Segundo, aged 11, Yaurisque, Peru)

If I have the right to play, I must let the others play with my things as well and so we become friends playing. I like playing. (Valia, aged 7, San Sebastian-Cusco, Peru)

If I have the right to go to school, I have to try my best in writing and reading. (Glicerio, aged 7, San Sebastian-Cusco, Peru)

Children from the Peruvian Andes, recorded for the local NGO CEARAS Kallpanchis.

Note

This work is based on one of the principles of the Global Ethic Foundation. This principle has existed in many religious and ethical traditions for thousands of years:

What you wish done to yourself, do to others.

In a world where space and time have been redefined by technolo gical advances and where the rich get richer every single day, the Foundation is convinced that changes are needed. It has used the Universal Declaration of Human Rights to formulate these four irrevocable directives:

Commitment to a culture of non-violence and respect for life

Commitment to a culture of solidarity and a just economic order

Commitment to a culture of tolerance and a life of truthfulness

Commitment to a culture of equal rights and partnership between men and women.

With thanks to Tim de Winter, former UNICEF consultant, for this activity, the examples from Peruvian children and the information on the Global Ethic Foundation.

Personal flags

Purpose

- To encourage children to think about what is important to them (CE)
- To help raise self-esteem (CE)
- To provide a medium for expressing personal identity that does not rely solely on writing (Art/CE)
- To allow for reflection on what lies behind countries' flags and symbols (G).

Preparation

You will need examples of flags and other symbols from around the world and plain A4 paper for each child and coloured pens

Procedures

Show children examples of flags and other national symbols. Can they recognise them? What do they represent? (e.g. Union Jack incorporates flags of four countries, U.S.A. flag incorporates the fifty-two states, Devon County symbol shows river and countryside). Discuss what they (or their family) might have on their own personal flag: demonstrate how they could divide their sheet into quarters with a symbol in each quarter, or perhaps have one symbol like Japan. Each child then draws his/her personal flag for display, writing a few lines of explanation to say 'I put these things on my flag because …'.

Plenary

- Are there some things we all had on our flags?
- What does this tell us about what we have in common?
- What did you learn about what is important to someone else?
- Do you think children in other countries would have the same things?
- What do flags and symbols tell us about places?

Possibilities

Children could go on to design a flag for the classroom, with symbols significant to the class, or design a flag for the school. This could be made in a textiles lesson. They could also discuss mottoes, and compose a motto to go with the personal, family or school flag. Older or more able children could be introduced to Latin and French mottoes.

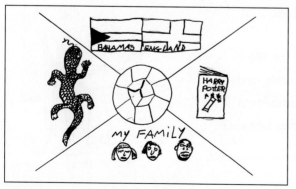

My personal flag. Theo, aged 11.

I put the 2 flags because I'm half Bahamian and half English and they are my countries. I put the Harry Potter books because they're the best books on earth, the football because my life revolves around it and my family because they are important to me. And of course my pet lizard because it's wicked.

In the news: rights denied, rights protected

Purpose

*   To help students recognise that human rights relate to everyday situations (CE)

*   To help students appreciate that whilst some people's rights are denied, organisations and individuals are working hard to ensure others' rights are protected (CE)

*   To help students understand the influence of the media (E, CE)

*   To encourage collaborative learning, speaking and listening (E, CE)

Preparation

You will need:

*   Old newspapers and magazines of all kinds, at least two for each group

*   A large sheet of sugar paper (or other A1 paper) for each group

*   Scissors and glue

*   A simplified version of the Universal Declaration of Human Rights (Handout 12)

Procedures

Explain to the group:

> *In our modern world more and more people have access to a large quantity of information than ever before. For most of us, this information comes through the media, and especially via the news. Everyday, TV screens, radios and newspapers are filled with situations and stories which are hopeful, tragic, happy, sad, simple or complex. Usually we look at the terrible news stories and feel powerless. However, by looking again, using the ideas of human rights, we can see patterns of success, where rights are protected and acted upon, and patterns of problems where rights are denied.*

Put students into groups of four or five and give each group a selection of newspapers and magazines. On the board draw a large circle. On the circumference of the circle write the following three phrases as far away from each other as possible: **rights denied, rights protected, rights in action**. The students copy this format on their large sheets.

Ask the groups to look through their newspapers and magazines to find things which illustrate each of the three phrases. These should be cut out and pasted near the relevant heading on the paper. Encourage the class to use all parts of the magazines and newspapers, including advertisements, classified adverts etc. You might need to help with some examples:

Rights denied

This could be an article complaining that a local health clinic has been closed without consulting the local community. This would illustrate the denial of the right to health or even life.

Rights protected

This could be a story about children who were rescued from people who were mistreating them.

Rights in action

This could be a picture of a footballer scoring a goal, illustrating the rights to leisure, health, freedom of association, or even travel.

When the group had completed the task (usually after 15 or 20 minutes) ask them to look at the simplified version of the Universal Declaration of Human Rights (UDHR) to find the article or articles which relate to the stories or pictures. Allow another 10 minutes for this activity. Now ask each group in turn to hold up their display (or Blu-tac on wall). As they do this they should explain why they chose these examples and which specific articles from the UDHR they illustrate.

Plenary

*   Which of the phrases was easiest to illustrate? Why?

*   Which was the most difficult? Why?

*   Were there any newspaper articles or other examples where all three phrases could be said to be relevant?

*   What groups work to protect the rights of others?

Possibilities

Students could go on to research in more depth groups actively working to protect the rights of others, e.g. Amnesty International, NSPCC. The work could be linked with a history topic, with students looking at newspaper extracts from that time. This could lead to a discussion of the rights of people in that particular historical period.

Adapted from Siniko – Towards a Human Rights Culture in Africa,
Index number AFR 01/03/99 Amnesty International Publications,
1 Easton St, London WC1X 0DW.

Summary of Universal Declaration of Human Rights.

Simplified by Amnesty International

Article 1

We are all born free.
We all have our own thoughts and ideas.
We shall all be treated in the same way.

Article 2

These rights belong to everybody, whatever our differences.

Article 3

We all have the right to life, and to live in freedom and safety.

Article 4

Nobody has any right to make us a slave and we cannot make anyone else our slave.

Article 5

Nobody has any right to hurt us or to torture us.

Article 6

We all have the same right to use the law.

Article 7

The law is the same for everyone. It must treat us all fairly.

Article 8

We can all ask for the law to help us when we are not fairly treated.

Article 9

Nobody has the right to put us in prison without good reason, to keep us there, or to send us away from our country.

Article 10

If we are put on trial, this should be in public. The people who try us should not let anyone tell them what to do.

Summary of Universal Declaration of Human Rights.

Simplified by Amnesty International

Article 11

Nobody should be blamed for doing something until it is proved. When people say we did a bad thing we have the right to show that it is untrue.

Article 12

Nobody should try to harm our good name. Nobody has the right to come into our home, open our letters, or bother us or our family without good reason.

Article 13

We all have the right to go wherever we want in our own country and travel abroad if we wish.

Article 14

If we are frightened of being badly treated in our own country, we all have the right to emigrate to another country for our own safety.

Article 15

We all have the right to citizenship of a country.

Article 16

Every adult has the right to marry and have a family if they wish. Men and women have the same rights when they are married as well as when they are separated.

Article 17

Everyone has the right to own things or share them. Nobody should take our possessions from us without a good reason.

Article 18

We all have the right to believe in whatever we wish, to have a faith and to change this if we wish.

Article 19

We all have the right to make up our own minds, to think what we like and to say what we think, as well as to share our ideas with other people.

Article 20

We all have the right to meet our friends and to work together in peace to defend our rights. Nobody can make us join a group if we don't want to.

Summary of Universal Declaration of Human Rights.

Simplified by Amnesty International

Article 21

We all have the right to take part in the government of our country. Every adult should be allowed to choose their own leaders.

Article 22

We all have the right to a home, enough money to live on, and medical help if we are ill. Music, art and craft, and sport should be for everyone to enjoy.

Article 23

Every adult has the right to a job, to a fair wage for their work and to join a trade union.

Article 24

We all have the right to rest from our work and to relax.

Article 25

We all have the right to enjoy a good life. Mothers, children, the elderly, the unemployed and the disabled have the right to be cared for.

Article 26

Education is a right, and primary school should be free. We should learn about the UN and how to co-operate with others. Our parents can choose what we learn.

Article 27

We all have the right to our own way of life, and to enjoy the good things that science and learning can bring.

Article 28

There must be political order and stability so that we can all enjoy rights and freedom not only in our own country but world wide.

Article 29

We have a duty to other people and we should protect their rights and freedom.

Article 30

Nobody can take away these rights and freedom from us.

Solve the mystery:
Why is Ranjesh's mum crying?

(The story used in this activity covers the suicide of a teenager who has been bullied. You are advised to use this with sensitivity to the particular needs of your students. The student's newspaper article (page 81) summarises the content of the story).

Purpose

• To provide opportunities to discuss race, religion and bullying (RE, PSHE)

• To foster collaborative groupwork and discussion skills (CE, E)

• To develop thinking skills, questioning connections, using prior knowledge and assumptions (CE, RE)

Preparation

You will need:

• a set of statements, (Handout 13) cut up, which make up Ranjesh's story for each group (put each group's set on different coloured card to prevent confusion). For special needs students reduce the number of cards so that you just leave them with the main story

• a whistle (the discussion can get loud and heated)

Procedure

Put the class into groups of between four and six. Explain that they are all detectives and they must use the clues in front of them to answer the question: Why is Ranjesh's mum crying? Explain that, as happens in reality, there may be some statements which are not relevant to the case. Allow them to work for about 10 minutes in groups, then draw them together (use the whistle if needed) and ask if they can solve the mystery. The answer you are looking for at this stage is that Ranjesh is dead so she is upset.

Now ask them to use the cards to construct the story and find out the reasons behind his death and the people connected to him. This group work will take about 20–25 minutes and you will need to walk around, listening and helping without giving direct answers. It does not matter how students connect the cards: some will make a spider diagram, others will make a list. It is the discussion that is important. Draw the class together for the plenary. Here you will need to ask open ended questions to develop the discussion. You can tailor the questions according to the focus you want as issues of bullying, religion and race are all covered in this 'mystery'.

Plenary

- How did Ranjesh die?
- What evidence do you have for saying this?
- What caused him to feel so bad?
- Why do you think Archie was bullying Ranjesh?
- What evidence do you have for saying this?
- How could Ranjesh have been helped? By whom?

Possibilities

The students could produce a newspaper front page reporting the story for homework. Ask students to write down how Ranjesh could/should have been helped: this might be useful when setting up an Anti-Bullying Policy. In religious education you could explore the issue of minority groups/faiths and their treatment. Students could look at the basic rights of all people to have a faith. You can of course write your own mystery: all you need is a story and a question.

With thanks to Sarah Leslie, Cullompton Community College.

(These activities were developed as part of the Thinking Skills project: see p. 135 in Chapter 7 for more details and for comments on using thinking skills in RE and geography).

Why is Ranjesh's mum crying?

Ranjesh has just turned 12 years old.

Ranjesh slept in a room with his younger brother.

The school did not have a good tutorial system.

Ranjesh and his friend Peter were in the same tutorial group.

Peter was worried about Ranjesh and his moods.

Mr Jones and Mrs Smith were worried about the aggressive nature of Archie and James.

Archie and his dad went to a meeting of the British National Party.

James was sick when he heard the news on Monday.

A turban is about two metres long and very strong.

Ranjesh sat for 2 hours and wrote down a 6-month diary of events.

Ranjesh's brother Deiter was hysterical and vowed he would never sleep in bunk beds again.

The head teacher, Mr Phillips, knew things would have to change.

Peter had never seen Ranjesh run so fast.

Claire felt that her boss hated her and gave her the worst jobs at work.

Mrs Groves was worried about the rise in the number of small coffins they had to make.

Archie had been beaten by his father.

Mrs Singh (Ranjesh's mum) thought Ranjesh was spending a lot of money.

Mrs Singh went to the temple with Ranjesh but he would not eat much. This worried her.

The Sikh leader commented to Mrs Singh that he had seen Ranjesh in a distressed state after school last week.

The school had a policy to tell on bullies.

Ranjesh was spending more time in his own room.

Childline's phone number is 0800 11 11 11.

Archie read the newspaper headline and laughed.

Archie hated it when people answered him back.

Peter went home one day with a black eye.

Archie's mum and dad never went to parents' evenings.

Mrs Singh was worried about the change in Ranjesh's report.

The Gazette

36p

Boy's bullying ordeal ends in tragedy

Ranjesh Singh, 12, committed suicide after bullying ordeal.

Yesterday a young lad (12) was found dead, hung to his bunk bed by his strong turban, which was about two meters long. A very distressed Mrs Singh found Ranjesh Singh's body Saturday night. The whole family of sikhs were shocked by this terrible incident. Ranjesh's younger brother who shared the same room as him swears that he will never sleep in a bunk bed again as long as he lives.

When Ranjesh's best fiend, Peter, found out about his sudden death he didn't look half as shocked as people thought he might be.

Peter who was in the same tutor group as Ranjesh told his mum and Mrs Singh that Ranjesh had been bullied at school. He also said, fighting back the tears, that he never thought that it would come to this. Peter's mum added that one night Peter came home with a black eye, which was probably connected with the bullying at school. In our interview with Peter he mentioned the two names Archie and James. These two boys were at the same school as Ranjesh and Peter and were involved with the bullying. Peter said he got the black eye after standing up for Ranjesh and his religion. He answered back to Archie, one of the bullies, who hated people answering him back so he punched Peter in the eye. Peter also spoke of the day when Ranjesh ran away from the bullies. He said he had never seen Ranjesh run so fast.

Archie was racist and was brought up to be like this by his parents. He and his dad went to the British National Front. This is a place where racist people go to talk about getting rid of people who they consider are different to them. Archie and Ranjesh's school said that Archie was beaten by his dad so he thought it was right to hurt people. The school also said that Archie's parents did not bother with Archie and school. The headteacher said that they have not been to one of Archie's parent evenings. After hearing the news of Ranjesh's death the headteacher knew he had to change the school rules. Lots of mums had said that they needed tutorials at the school to teach the kids about bullying and rights and wrongs. It is awful that things had to go this far until the school decided that it would be a good idea.

Mrs Singh said that Ranjesh had been spending more time alone in his room and acting a bit unusual and that made her and her husband worry. She also said that he was not eating as much as usual when they went out. Mrs Singh had a slight feeling that Ranjesh might have been bullied when all his dinner money went missing. At the time she thought nothing of it.

After Ranjesh's death Mrs Singh found a piece of paper in his room with a number on it. The number turned out to be the childline number. She also found Ranjesh's diary in his room. It had the last six months of his life written in it. Mrs Singh said reading it made her understand all the problems he was going through but also made her really upset. She still can't come to terms with what has happened to her son. She thought he was happy. The coffin makers said that they could not believe how many small coffins they have been making. They think that it is terrible that the amounts of young deaths are so high.

School children that know Ranjesh say that they are so upset and that Ranjesh was always nice and friendly. The main bully Archie just laughed at the newspaper but his mate James looked as if he was about to be sick.

This is all the news we have on this terrible tragedy but we are still finding out more about how it happened.

If you or anyone you know is being bullied talk to someone about it and get it sorted before it is too late.

CHILDLINE phone no.: 0800 1111 11

Newspaper article by Laura Newcombe, Year 9, Cullompton Community College.

81

6

Teaching about Democracy: Political Literacy

Everyone should respect one another, because if they don't, communities will fall apart. If you nick the farmers' crops or livestock you will be starved for three days. (Our laws for Mesopotamia: Jack and Caragh aged 9)

A bad citizenship programme, a boring one based on something like learning the constitution, might do more harm than good. (Crick, TES 4/09/98)

I see quite a few young people who are in serious trouble. One of the problems is that they don't understand about rights and responsibilities. They come to me demanding their rights but what they don't realise is that when they break a law they're infringing the rights of others. (Barrister)

Introduction

Teaching about democracy, democratic processes and the legal system has consistently been a difficult area for teachers. Some teachers feel that 'politics' has no place in the classroom, others worry that their own understanding is not sufficient. For many years this area has been marginalised in the curriculum. However, a healthy democracy requires active citizens who are informed about the work of local, national and European governments and their role in supporting democratic processes. Parallel to this, young people need a basic understanding of law and justice. This will entail understanding that the law protects as well as prosecutes, and that in order to have rights we also have responsibilities.

Key issues

Living in a democracy

How do we help students acquire knowledge and understanding about systems of government and decision-making? How can we make such complex information accessible? How can we model democratic processes in the teaching of democracy? What can we learn from democracies in the past?

Understanding justice and the law

How can we help students understand some basic aspects of the legal system? How can we help them understand that the law is constantly evolving? How can we ensure that students appreciate that whilst the law is there to protect them, they also have a responsibility to respect the rights of others?

Recent research findings

Living in a democracy

Previous attempts to teach political literacy to children in the 8–13 age range have met with resistance from teachers. Harwood, researching into teachers' practice for the World Studies 8–13 project, found that they ignored this aspect of the work and consistently rated political skills as unimportant (1984). Yet Stevens's (1982) research with primary school children indicates that from the age of seven onwards, they are 'able to take part intelligently in discussion about politics' and from nine, can discuss 'concepts of democracy, leadership and accountability of government' (p. 168). However, it was not until the Crick report (QCA, 1998) which underpins the new National Curriculum for Citizenship Education, that there was renewed interest in teaching about democracy. This report draws on a number of recent surveys to support the teaching of political literacy. Crewe's (1996) research reveals the disengagement of British pupils from discussion of public and political issues. Wilkinson and Mulgan (1995) present evidence of ignorance and an increased 'disrespect for the way parliament works' (p. 16). But the advisory group warns that it is not merely a return to the teaching of the British constitution that is needed. It appreciates that young people <u>are</u> interested in particular political issues (e.g. environmental issues) and in improving their local community, and recommends that we equip students with 'the political skills needed to change laws in a peaceful and responsible manner' (p. 10) with regard to both local and national issues.

This approach reflects some of the principles endorsed by Huckle, a long-standing advocate of the need for political education (1996). He cites protests over road constructions and live animal exports as examples of 'the appeal of cultural politics amongst the young and its power to build new alliances in changed times' (p. 34). Drawing on Gilbert (1995), Huckle argues that cultural politics is a necessary aspect of citizenship education and that this may in fact be the key to gaining students' interest. Through this we can link abstract rights to everyday life and can look to expanded models of democracy.

Understanding justice and the law

Osler (1998) worked with 16–18-year-olds to assess their levels of understanding of four broad categories of rights: social and economic rights, legal rights, political or participatory rights and children's protection rights. Her research showed that out of the four categories, there was a much lower level of interest and understanding about legal rights and a lack of sympathy from many of the students for the rights of juvenile offenders. Osler concludes that young people are 'ill-informed and ill-equipped' and that there may be a particular need to develop students' understanding of legal frameworks and their contribution to the protection of human rights.

Talbot and Tate (1997) recommend that children be taught values which include respecting 'the rule of law and encouraging others to do so'. Clough's work with student teachers (1998) indicates, however, that this group gave a relatively low value to democratic and legal processes when faced with another of Talbot and Tate's recommendations, accepting 'responsibility to maintain a sustainable environment'. Seventy per cent of students in Clough's research agreed that sometimes citizens are 'right to break the law to protect the environment' (p. 71). While this reflects the importance of 'single issue' politics to young people, it also indicates the complexity of teaching about conflicting rights, the law and the role of peaceful protest. Such complexity should not mean that teaching about justice and the law is ignored, but rather that teachers are given clear guidelines so that they can help children form their own opinions based on an understanding of democratic processes, justice and the law.

Activities: Teaching about the concept of democracy

Key points about democracy

These basic principles of democracy can stand as information for the teacher or can be used with older students to demonstrate that democracy is a concept involving much more than majority rule. They could also be used as a diamond ranking exercise for older students or staff. Participants should be asked to rank the statements, putting the statement they think is most important at the top, and so on (see p. 55 in Chapter 4 for an example of how to carry out a diamond ranking exercise).

1 A core definition

The word democracy has many meanings, but in the modern world it means that the ultimate authority in political affairs rightfully belongs to citizens. This is because the government has been elected by the majority of the adults governed. It is based on the view that most human beings are responsible, that their views deserve recognition and respect and that they have a right to choose their government.

2 A matter of degree

In any democracy there are debates about who can vote and old democracies like the U.K. have 'undemocratic' features, for example, a hereditary monarch as Head of State.

3 Freely given consent

If a government is to be elected by the people of the country, the people must have what is called 'freely given consent'. This means adults may vote for the party of their choice without fear of violence or threats. It also means there must be freedom of speech for the press.

4 Participation

Participation in a democracy is essential as otherwise individuals may become disinterested. We regard a country as democratic if all adults are able to vote, regardless of race, gender, religion, or property.

5 Parliamentary democracy

The parliamentary system of government is followed in Britain. The voters elect members of parliament (MPs). These members in turn, elect a prime minister who chooses ministers for his cabinet from the MPs.

6 Democracy and the press

It is especially difficult to define the role of the press and other mass media in a democratic society. Ideally, a free press should be responsible to truth, balanced, fair, and careful to distinguish between reports of fact and statements of political opinion. However, this does not always happen as newspapers can try to sway people's opinions by what they choose to print.

7 Checks and balances

In a representative democracy, government is checked in many ways – for example there may be two elected assemblies or national and regional governments.

8 Pressure groups

Another important way of checking government is by forming pressure groups to protect interests and causes – whether in the workplace (for example, trade unions) or as concerned citizens (for example, the RSPCA).

9 Arguments against democracy

Some people argue that most human beings are not intelligent enough to choose who should govern and that good government is so complex that only a few people are capable of doing it. But if this is the case, who will control the government?

Further possibilities for teaching about democracy

1   Students can be asked to research newspapers or the internet for contemporary debates – e.g. fox hunting, legalisation of soft drugs, animal rights, AIDS, cloning, etc. The aim is to inform students of the complexities of issues and the key factor that people of intelligence and goodwill can be found on both sides of any issue. Class debates after research are an excellent way of bringing out differences, argument and counter-argument and engaging students in voting.

2   Pressure groups are an essential part of a democracy. What do specific pressure groups stand for, what are their goals, their tactics, who are they opposing? Students' interests can be harnessed – who represents professional footballers, fishermen, doctors, students?

3   Political parties: what are the party's philosophies? What are their policies? Who are their leaders?

4   Institutions and parliament: what is Prime Minister's Question Time? What does the Speaker do? What powers does the monarch have? Should the monarchy be reformed or abolished?

5   The media: what political disputes are recorded in today's newspapers? Do different newspapers have a bias?

With thanks to Ian Wright,
Head of Politics, Exeter School.

85

Magna Carta: charter for freedom

The Magna Carta is such an important document that it could be referred to in assemblies when introducing school councils or school rules, using the basic information below. Alternatively it can be used as part of a history topic as suggested here.

Purpose

- To introduce students to this charter which is the basis of English law (H, CE)

- To raise students' awareness of the responsibilities of leadership (H, CE)

- To help students appreciate the effect this has had on our lives today (CE)

Preparation

You will need different sources of information about King John, the roles of the barons and bishops and copies of the Magna Carta. There are significant aspects which students need to understand.

- A charter is a list of promises requested by those with less power (or on behalf of these groups), which the more powerful are being asked to keep.

- The Magna Carta was a very important charter – it listed sixty-four promises for King John to keep

- The barons made these demands on the basis of four complaints about King John's behaviour:

  1 He had lost lands in France

  2 He demanded high taxes to pay for these wars

  3 He ill-treated his people, through torture and violence

  4 He quarrelled with the church and had been excommunicated.

- The 39th clause is important as it outlines a basic right:

    No freeman shall be arrested, imprisoned, or have his property taken away, or be outlawed, or exiled, or in any way ruined, except by lawful judgement or by the law of the land.

- The Magna Carta was updated and it later became part of the law of the land

    It was the first written programme of political reform ever imposed on an English King by his subjects.

    (Saul, N., 1983, *The Companion to Medieval England*)

Procedure

As a whole class, ask students to consider what skills are required in an effective leader. They could look towards respected teachers/people within the community/ in the media, whose qualities they admire. Then ask what extra qualities a leader of a country should have. Generate a 'spider diagram' on the board.

Group work: King John as leader

Next, focus on the story of King John. Tell students that they will study a leader who perhaps lacked many of the qualities that they perceive as being important. Give alternative groups information on the barons and bishops. Based on this, students must produce a charter of five demands from the position of baron or bishop detailing change. Then ask students to move next to someone with a different viewpoint, so that barons and bishops work together. Together they will re-write a final charter on which they both agree. Bring the class back together, and have the pairs report back on their charters. Then show your students the main points contained within the actual Magna Carta (1215).

Plenary

- Why did King John sign the Magna Carta?

- What does this tell us about good leadership?

- How do you think that Magna Carta affects our lives today? (political freedom/democratic process)

- What other kinds of charter do you know about?

Possibilities

The teacher could go on to look at how laws are made now, key laws since the Magna Carta and the role of parliament. This could be extended to include a European dimension by looking at how the French kings dealt with the demands to change up to 1789. Students can find out about other charters through which people have created a list of demands calling for a change in the way certain groups of citizens are treated by leaders. This links well with the activities in Chapter 5 on the Universal Declaration of Human Rights and the Rights of the Child.

With thanks to Nicola Clay,
Plymstock School.

Current issues: put it to the cabinet

Purpose

- To help students understand how Parliament works (CE)

- To demonstrate the work of cabinet ministers and their departments (CE)

- To link the work of government to current events (CE)

Preparation

You will need information about Parliament (e.g. education sheets provided free of charge from Parliament Education Unit www.parliament.uk) and newspaper cuttings relating to such issues as health, transport, education, international news.

Procedure

Initial discussion with whole class: what is Parliament? Who is our prime minister? What is an MP? How many are there? Who is our MP? What does he/she do? Give out information as necessary (e.g. there are currently 657 MPs, the main work of Parliament is to make laws, debate current affairs and examine the work of the government and proposals from the EU).

Then ask what the difference is between Parliament and the government. Explain that while Parliament is composed of all elected MPs, the government is made up from the political party which won the last election and its most senior members are the cabinet. This is like the senior management of the school. Just as a school has a head of mathematics, head of history etc., the cabinet has people responsible for different areas. There are about twenty-four cabinet members. In twos, students should see if they can identify ten possible areas that cabinet members could be in charge of. Collect their ideas and explain that some of the departments are:

- education and employment

- home affairs

- agriculture, fisheries and food

- health

- culture, media and sport

- defence

- foreign affairs

- transport

Do they know who any of the current ministers for these departments are? Explain that ministers often only stay in their post for four years and that they are informed by civil servants who may work for a lifetime in one department. In groups, students should examine newspaper cuttings about current issues and decide which government department would need to deal with each one. They select which they think is the most pressing issue and write a short statement to the cabinet minister responsible requesting action or money.

Plenary

Groups report back

* Which issues did you think were important? Why?

* Of all the issues in the papers, which is most important in the long term?

* What kind of arguments might persuade a cabinet minister to take action?

* Can governments solve all problems? Why? Why not?

Students can then use the website www.number-10.gov.uk/default.asp?pageid=8 and put questions to the cabinet minister currently on line.

Possibilities

'If I was elected . . .': tell students they have just been elected as an MP, but in order to have the chance to put forward a 'bill' proposing a change in the law, they must first be able to survive as an MP. It is like the first day at a new school. They must find out where they should sit, how many other MPs there are in their party, what the 'whips' are, and what happens when the division bell rings. Then they can start on the real business of being an MP and think what it is they would like to bring to Parliament's attention in their maiden speech. (Ambitious students can decide what they would do if they were prime minister and submit their proposals to the website above.)

'A day in the life of . . .': many people are unsure about what MPs actually do. Get students to canvas opinion on this. They can ask teachers, parents and others in the community what they think their MP does and should do. On the basis of this, draw up a list of statements about what the class thinks an MP does and some further questions, and either send these to your local MP or invite him/her into the school.

We remember: symbols and identity

Purpose

- To help students understand the role of symbols as indicators of both past and present (H, CE)
- To foster discussion on the importance of symbols to different communities and the need to respect these (CE, RE)
- To help students understand that symbols and traditions change (CE)
- To design new symbols (CE, Art, D&T)

Preparation

You will need:

- symbols of state and government. e.g. flag, coat of arms, stamps, banknotes
- symbols of national commemoration, e.g. poppies, Jubilee mug
- symbols from the local area, e.g. county/town logo, local conservation group
- symbols important to individuals, e.g. swimming badge, family crest

Procedure

Establish that these symbols are or were important to people for a reason. Ask why they think they are (or were) important and be prepared to explain the meaning of each one. Ask the class as a whole to try to group the items according to whom they are important, or what they show. You can use the four groups above or have students identify their own. Record the decisions on a board/flip chart. Then discuss:

Which symbols tell us about the past?

Which tell us about who has power?

Which tell us something about our country?

Which of these symbols do you think will be still here in 100 years?

Which do you think should still be here in 100 years?

Task: In twos or threes, design a new logo or emblem either for your country, town or local community. How can you make it reflect both past and present?

Plenary

- What are the characteristics of a memorable symbol?
- Why is it important to have symbols?
- Should we respect symbols of the past? Why? Why not?

- What if some symbols are considered offensive now (e.g. Nazi insignia)? Should these be banned?

- How do symbols help us understand our identity as a community or nation?

Possibilities

This work could be extended to look at people behind the symbols, e.g. the people on banknotes (Who are they? What did they do?). Students could also look at national monuments, national songs and events (e.g. bonfire night) and examine the stories behind these. This could lead to discussion on the invention of tradition and the importance of tradition to all societies.

Political action: campaigning for change

Purpose

- To help students appreciate that there are many different ways of campaigning for change, both inside and outside the law (CE)

- To help students learn about different courses of action that people have taken in relation to local issues (H, G)

- To teach the skills of listening and advocacy (E, CE)

- To help students to feel confident to make informed judgments about different political actions (CE).

Preparation

You will need a sheet (Handout 14) providing background information about the building of the A30 Honiton bypass and role cards (Handout 15) for each group of people.

Procedure

With the whole class, have an initial discussion about some of the controversial campaigns that are current (e.g. preventing medical research on animals). Brainstorm ways that people may make their feelings heard about such issues (letters to press, to MPs, protests, etc.) and establish that there are many different ways of expressing opinions, some of which may be legal and some of which may involve breaking the law.

Explain that today they are going to look at a real example of a controversial issue where people took different forms of political action. Give the class the background to the building of the Honiton bypass (Handout 14). Explain that it made the national news because not everyone agreed with the decisions of the government to build the road. Many people campaigned both for and against the new road and a group of mainly young people took political action in their own way. Divide the class into groups representing:

- Sheriff and local police

- Local residents

- Animals (primary only!)

- Protestors

- Road builders

- Children and teachers of the nearby primary school

- Department of Transport and the Environment

- News team (this is best played by the teacher with younger children)

Each group has a card detailing who they are and what they stand for (Handouts 14 and 15). Explain that after fifteen minutes they are all going to assume their roles at the place where the road is being built. They will be asked to stand in position as a tableau (i.e. frozen in action) and then will unfreeze as BBC news interviewers come to their group. They will then have 3 minutes to explain their particular point of view to the news team. The members of the group must be ready to explain their views on the building of the road, what action they have taken or are about to take (if any) and why they have done this. As the news team visits each group in turn, the members of the group 'unfreeze' and put their case. The interviewers can also ask 'probing' questions.

Plenary

- How did it feel to have to represent a certain group (especially if their opinions differed from yours)?

- What must you consider in order to make a good case?

- In what way did the values of the different groups vary?

- Did anyone change his/her mind as a result of hearing another point of view?

- Which groups were acting outside the law? Was this right?

- What kinds of action can people take legally?

- What would you do if this situation arose in your area?

Possibilities

If this activity is being done with secondary students, it is probably advisable to replace the 'animals' with a group of adults/children who are there to protect the rights of the animals (primary children are usually happy to role-play animals: this is reminiscent of 'Farthing Wood' where animals were hounded from their habitat by builders and 'spoke' about their escape).

This activity can also be extended to further role-play and drama. Prior to preparing their arguments for the news team, the groups can have 10 minutes to circulate in the classroom, so that they can question others about their viewpoint, lobby each other and exchange views.

Case study

Children in the primary school close to the bypass worked on a project such as the one indicated in the role play above (but did not get interviewed by the BBC!). Interviews with the children indicated how this work developed their thinking from the early stages when the head teacher had thought that many supported and identified with the protestors. By the end of the project many had a greater understanding of the various routes open for political action. Three children commented:

More roads may mean that there will be more cars. The protestors did not have the right to trespass, but I do think that they have the right to protest.

I have learnt you can protest in different ways, for example by writing a letter. Protesting can be very civilised, through talking and negotiating. You don't have to use force to stop something.

I've learnt that people will go to extreme levels to stop another person doing something they don't want to happen. The protestors could have killed themselves. The tunnels were not supported properly.

Through being involved in the arguments and counter-arguments, the children began to develop social and structural insights and to express an understanding of values and action. In addition, their concern for the environment was matched by a corresponding concern for democratic processes.

(See Clough (1998) for a fuller description of this primary school's work).

Background Information

During the academic year of 1996–7, children in a small primary school in a Devon village found that they had a new community living on their doorstep – a community of protestors against the building of a new high road through 'Fair Mile' to provide relief for the overstretched A30 route between Honiton and Exeter. A teacher in the school commented:

The impact of traffic on the road had worsened in the past few years. The pressure was felt throughout the year, not just in the summer months. There had been bad accidents and people had been killed. At the same time it was a beautiful location. Nearly all the local people wanted a new road, but not through or near their village. Farmers were anxious about their land. There was a fear that the new road would attract more traffic. The protest was not violent. There was no damage to property. Locals were impressed that the protestors were prepared to put their lives on the line. But they were seen as outsiders.

After much media interest and a delay of several weeks, the protestors were removed peacefully and the road was built. The protestors moved on to other sites where they campaigned for the environment in a similar way and Swampy, their spokesperson, became, for a short time, a well-known figure.

Role cards

> *The sheriff and local police*
> Your group is the local police, with one of you being the sheriff. It is your duty to carry out the law which means you must move the protestors who are obstructing the road builders. You don't want to use violence, so you need to think how to persuade them to leave their trees and tunnels peacefully. The sheriff has to explain to the protestors that they are trespassing and this is against the law. Your group wants the press (news team) to understand that you are there to enforce the law.

> *Local residents*
> Some of you are for the road and some against, although you all agree that the current road is very congested. One of you had a good friend killed in an accident on the current road and you want the new road built. Another of you wants the road built but for it to take another route so that this stretch of woodland is preserved. Another thinks the new wider road will only attract more traffic. You have to see if you can agree a case to put to the press.

Role cards

The animals (primary children only)

You are aware of what is happening – you have seen the bulldozers and you know what this means. You are worried about losing your habitat, your hedges, trees, streams and open fields. If you move to a new area you will be harassed by other animals who live there. Can you make yourselves seen on the TV? Can you alert viewers to what is happening?

The protestors

You feel strongly that too much of Britain is being covered in concrete, that there are too many roads and that some beautiful places are being destroyed. You feel that animals have rights as well as humans. You are living in tunnels you have dug across the pathway that the bulldozers are clearing. You don't feel that writing letters to politicians or newspapers does any good and you are prepared to risk your lives to save this piece of woodland. You believe that press coverage will help your cause.

The road builders

Your job is to build roads and you want to get on with what you have been paid to do. Some of you support the new road as you feel that there has been a public consultation and people have had a chance to make their views heard, so the road should be built. Others are worried about the protestors being hurt if there is a violent confrontation and have some sympathy for their view. You don't really want to speak to the press: you just want to get on with your job.

The teachers of the nearby school

You are aware of what is going on and feel that the children in your school ought to be informed about controversial local issues. You have decided to let your pupils do a project on the new road, interviewing parents, the local sheriff and others. However you are worried that parents will think that teaching about the protest might encourage children to join in (as some local teenages have done already). The news team has heard about your work and comes to find out more. Be prepared to defend your work.

The Department of Transport and the Environment

You have carried out all the correct procedures. There has been an inquiry into the building of the road, objections have been listened to and some amendments to the original plans made. The scheme has been costed and you wish it to go ahead. You feel annoyed that some people have decided they are 'above the law' and have put their own lives at risk as well as those of the police. You are also annoyed about the costs to taxpayer caused by this protest. You wish the matter to be resolved quickly.

Activities: understanding justice and the law

What happens when...?
The law and people involved

Purpose

- To encourage students to think about the consequences of crime (CE)

- To provide basic information about the procedures which take place after arrest (CE)

- To provide information about the roles of the various people involved (CE)

- To facilitate discussion and co-operative working (CE, E)

Preparation

You will need:

- copies of 'Whose job is it?' and 'Sequence of events' (Handouts 16 and 17)

- an OHT of the flow diagram (Handout 18)

Procedure

Ask the class if they know what happens to someone of 16 who commits a crime. Establish a definition of 'crime'. Elicit their level of understanding about the different outcomes and who might be involved in deciding what the young person's punishment should be.

Group work: give out a set of statements (Handout 16) to each group and explain that they must match each person against their role. This should only take each group about 5 minutes, after which check their understanding. Explain that the next task is to arrange the second set of statements (Handout 17) in a flow diagram to show the various consequences of a 16-year-old committing a crime. Allow 10 or 15 minutes (you could give younger children a blank outline of the flow diagram to help them).

Plenary

Check the understanding of the class as a whole, and ensure that all have the right sequence of events. Use Handout 18. Check understanding of the legal vocabulary.

- Does anyone know a police officer, magistrate or barrister?

- Are you surprised at what can happen to a 16-year-old who commits a crime?

(continued on page 100)

Whose job is it?

Barrister or solicitor	This person will ask you about what has happened, advise you and defend you
Police officer	This person is responsible for arresting and interviewing you
Magistrate	If your case is less serious, this person hears your case. He/she decides whether or not you are guilty and passes sentence on you.
Probation officer	This person supervises certain types of sentence and tries to rehabilitate you in the community.
Judge	This person hears your case, if it is more serious. A jury will decide whether or not you are guilty, but this person will pass sentence.
Prison officer	This person ensures that you stay locked up and tries to rehabilitate you.

The sequence of events

Arrested by the police	Community penalties (supervision, attendance centres)
Prison	Less serious offence tried in youth court
Police keep a record of the offence	Acquitted (not guilty)
Interviewed by police (entitled to lawyer and adult)	Conditional discharge and/or fine
Cautioned (formal warning)	Parents notified
Community penalties (supervision, attendance centres)	Prison
Conditional discharge and/or fine	16-year-old commits a crime
Prosecuted (taken to court)	Acquitted (not guilty)
Serious offence tried at Crown Court	

Possible sequence of events.

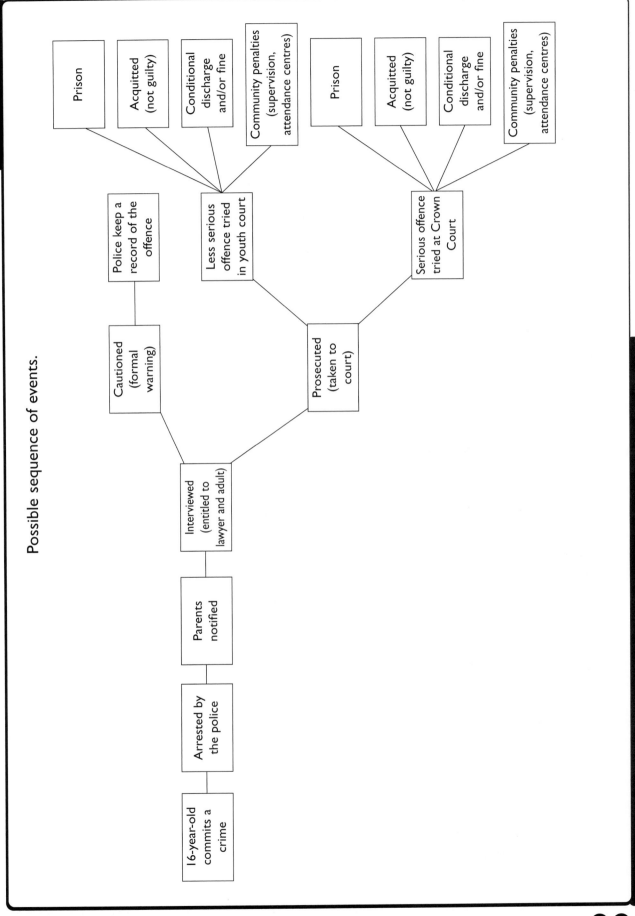

- What do you think would be a fair community service?

- Why do you think a person's crime is recorded even if they are not sent to prison?

- Why is a young person entitled to a lawyer when they are interviewed?

- Do you think our legal system is fair? Why or why not?

Possibilities

The students could go on to look at the job of judges and magistrates or to study what goes on in court. A police officer could be invited to talk to the class. The class could discuss what falls into the category of 'less serious' and 'more serious' crimes. They could compare the criminal justice systems in different countries and the different penalties for crimes. They could also look at what happens to children under 16.

Rights and laws

Purpose

- To provide students with information about some basic rights and laws (CE)

- To help students understand the complexity of the law (CE)

- To stimulate discussion about the reasons for laws (rights and protection) (CE)

- To help students appreciate that the legal system is constantly evolving (CE)

Preparation

You will need one set of the statements (Handout 19) for each group of students. Each group will need a sheet of A4 paper with two large overlapping circles drawn on it, with the headings 'agree' on one circle, 'disagree' on the other circle, and 'not sure' where the circles intersect.

Procedure

Explain to the students that they are going to work in groups to look at a list of statements about some basic laws and rights of people in the U.K. Some of these statements are true, others are false. In their groups, they must decide whether each statement is true or false, giving their reasons for their decision. After 15 minutes, gather the students together and elicit from them which statements they thought were true, and which false. Correct any misunderstandings, explaining the correct version of the statements listed below.

Then ask the students in their groups to select seven of the statements which provided the most discussion in their group and write these out, changing the wording if they were 'false' statements so that they are now 'true'. For example, the statement 'A child of 9 who kills someone can go to jail' would be changed to 'A child of 9 who kills someone cannot go to jail as they are under the age of criminal responsibility'. 'Cannabis use is illegal except for medical reasons' would be changed to 'Cannabis use is illegal'. They must then cut out these statements and place them in one of the circles on the prepared A4 sheets, according to whether they agree, disagree or are 'not sure'. In order to ensure that each student gets the opportunity to voice his/her own opinion, it is recommended that you advise students to look at one statement at a time, with people taking it in turns to say if they agree/disagree with the statements and why. If there are statements in the 'not sure' intersection, you can ask students to suggest amendments to these laws so that they do agree with them.

Plenary

* How well did your group 'know the law'?

* Which laws protect young people?

* Were there any laws/rights which everyone agreed with (supports)?

* Which were you not sure about? Why?

* Are there some laws which you feel should be changed? Why?

* Who would benefit if they were changed? Would anyone lose out?

Possibilities

Students could be encouraged to find out more about the rights of children (see Chapter 5) and about the making of laws. They need to understand that whilst everyone has rights, these come with responsibilities, so work on laws could be extended to look at how someone who breaks the law infringes the rights of others.

Right and laws: true/false

1   You can get married at 16.

2   You can legally have sex with someone of the opposite sex at 15.

3   You can buy fireworks from the age of 14.

4   Every child has the right to a free education.

5   Every child must attend school.

6   Heroin use is illegal.

7   Cannabis use is illegal except for medical reasons.

8   Rastafarians are allowed to use cannabis for religious and cultural reasons.

9   It is always illegal to carry a knife in a public place.

10   You can carry a knife for self-defence.

11   Parents can be fined for their children's criminal activities.

12   A child of 12 can be held responsible for a criminal offence if it can be proved that they knew what they were doing was wrong.

13   A child of 9 who kills someone can go to jail.

14   A child can take action to live apart from his/her parents.

15   Anyone is presumed to be innocent unless he/she is proved guilty.

16   A jury has the right to know about someone's previous convictions.

17   You can buy alcoholic drinks in a pub from the age of 18.

18   You can get a part-time job from the age of 13, but not in school hours.

19   You have the right to retaliate (hit back).

20   You have the right to retaliate on the sports field.

Rights and laws: answers

1 True

2 False. The age of consent is 16.

3 False. You can buy fireworks without an adult present at 16.

4 True.

5 False. Parents have the right to 'educate otherwise' their children, subject to inspection of their provision.

6 True.

7 False. All use of cannabis is illegal (but there are calls to change this and there is a derivative of cannabis available for medical use).

8 False – as above.

9 False. You may carry a knife if there is 'good reason', e.g. you are a builder or cook.

10 False. This is hardly ever held to be a 'good reason'.

11 True.

12 True. The boys who murdered Jamie Bulger (1993) were 10 at the time and deemed to be able to understand the difference between right and wrong.

13 False. The age of criminal responsibility is 10.

14 True, although this happens very rarely.

15 True.

16 False. A judge will have this information and will refer to it when passing sentence, but a jury has to judge on the facts alone and not on someone's background.

17 True.

18 True.

19 False. The concept of self-defence is complex, but generally you only have the right to prevent yourself from being hit (again) if it is necessary to defend yourself and the force you use is reasonable.

20 False. The law applies equally on the sports field as off.

Why do some people break the law?

103

Dilemmas and the law

Purpose

- To help students understand the role of the legal system when the rights of people are in conflict (CE)

- To give students the opportunity to voice their own opinions and consider their own values (E, CE, RE)

- To enable students to appreciate that there are often many sides to an argument (CE, PSHE)

Preparation

You will need examples of case studies of legal dilemmas. Two are provided: case study A (the conjoined twins) and case study B (the rights of the killers of Jamie Bulger to anonymity).

Procedure

Give half the class copies of case study A and the other half copies of case study B. Explain that both of these case studies came about because there were no obvious 'right answers' and in each case there were two groups of people whose interests were in conflict. In case A, the right of one child to life was in conflict with the right of the other. In case B, the rights of the boys (now young men) to rehabilitation were in conflict with the rights of the public to know where individuals who have committed an offence are living. Ask students to read the case studies individually and then in small groups draw up a list with two columns to show both sides of the argument. They should discuss as a group whether they agree with the judge's decision (and why or why not). Each group should select a spokesperson to report back on their particular case study and the main points of their discussion.

Plenary

- Why were these both such difficult decisions?

- What were the arguments for and against separating the twins in case A?

- What were the arguments for and against giving the boys anonymity in case B?

- Do you agree with the final decisions?

- What would happen if we did not have a legal system to make these decisions?

- Are there any other examples of moral and ethical dilemmas?

Possibilities

Students could study other cases where a legal decision has set a precedent, e.g. the case of Donoghue v Stephenson where the remains of a snail found in a bottle of ginger beer led to the ruling that a person with a responsibility for others (e.g. a manufacturer) who does not take sufficient care may have to compensate anyone he has harmed. Work could also be done on the roles of various legal bodies and institutions, e.g. the High Court, the Court of Appeal, magistrates courts, etc.

Case study A

In 2000, conjoined twin girls were born. One of the girls, Mary, was much weaker and drew her blood supply from her twin sister, Jodie. If the girls were not separated both would die. If they were separated Mary would definitely die whereas Jodie would have the chance of life although there were doubts about whether this would be of a 'high quality'. The parents, Catholics from the island of Gozo, initially argued that nature should be allowed to take its course and both girls should be allowed to die. The case ended up eventually at the Court of Appeal, where three judges had to make a decision. One of them, Lord Justice Ward, said it was 'the most awful dilemma to contemplate. Say "Yes" and you murder Mary. Say "No" and you murder Jodie'. In effect the judges had to consider the right of one life against another, and also consider the wishes of the parents. The judges finally ruled that the girls should be separated. Once this decision had been made the parents supported it and the operation to separate the girls took place. Mary died and Jodie survived.

Case study B

In 1993 two boys, aged 10, abducted Jamie Bulger (aged 2) from outside a shop, walked him through a shopping centre on to nearby wasteland and murdered him. The case caused widespread shock because of the age of the boys: people were surprised that children could commit such a terrible crime. There was much discussion about whether poor parenting, horror videos or a general lack of values in society was to blame or whether the boys were just 'evil'. They were given a 'life sentence', which also caused a huge debate as some people thought they were too young to be punished in this way.

In early 2001 the boys, now young men, were due for release. Dame Butler-Sloss, Britain's most senior family judge, granted them anonymity for life by issuing a permanent injunction referring to the new Human Rights Act (Article 1: the right to life). This was done to protect the young men after threats of revenge attacks. This is the first time the media has been permanently prevented from publishing information about convicted young offenders and some newspapers felt this went against the principle of the freedom of the press and the public's right to know about such people. The injunction has, however, been welcomed by the detectives involved and others who want the young men to have a chance to live normal lives.

Earlier societies: laws and justice

Purpose

*   To extend students' understanding of the laws and government of earlier societies (H, CE)
*   To provide opportunities for students to debate the need for laws and justice (CE, H)
*   To help students work collaboratively to resolve conflicts of interest (CE)

Preparation

You will need large sheets of paper (two for each group) and information on the laws of that society.

Procedure

Introduce the class to the concept of government. Explain that all societies need rules and laws, but that often it is difficult to decide on laws that are fair to everyone and those who make the laws have a great deal of power. A just society is one where the interests of all its people are taken into account.

Explain that for the purpose of this activity they are going to be divided into groups with each group representing one interest group (e.g. farmers). Divide class into groups. Ensure that they know what each group does to earn its living and what its main role is. Each group then has 20 minutes to come up with what they feel should be the laws of that country (at that time in history) and why. (You could ask them to think about who should vote, who should pay taxes, who has rights, what might happen if someone commits a crime.) They must bear in mind the interests of the other groups and what they know about that society at that time. Their laws should be written on the first of the large sheets of paper.

After 20 minutes call the groups together and ask one person from each group to share what they have written. Put the sheets on the wall for reference.

*   Has each group looked after their own interests first?
*   Are some of the laws for the common good?

Then regroup the students so that one person from each group meets with one from each of the other groups to form five or six new groups. As a group composed of people representing all the interest groups in that society they must now come to a consensus on the rules and laws for the benefit of all, using the second large sheet of paper.

After a further 30 minutes, share findings and if time, refer to the actual laws of that society.

Plenary

*   What were the problems in trying to decide a common set of laws?
*   Which of the laws and rights do you consider fair to all?

- Which interest groups felt excluded?

- How do your laws compare to those in existence at the time?

- Which of the laws that you wrote do we have now in the U.K.?

- Would you have liked to live under that system of law? Why or why not?

Possibilities

Future lessons can look in more depth at the system of government and the laws of the society. Work can be done on specific people in that period of history who reformed the law or worked for a more just society and students can look at our current laws and how these differ.

Case study

Year 5/6: Mesopotamia – laws and government

A class of Year 5/6 children had been studying Mesopotamia (Ancient Sumer), one of the world history studies suggested in the National Curriculum. The teacher wanted her children to understand how early societies developed their laws and systems of government. She thought this history study was particularly appropriate as the Code of Hammurabi, created in about 1800 B.C., has 282 laws (carved in stone) which are some of the earliest laws in existence.

The teacher followed the lesson plan above. The class were divided initially into five groups: farmers and fishermen, craftspeople, scribes, slaves and nobles. The children knew about the roles of each group but less about the Sumerian's system of law. The teacher wanted the children to consider what kind of laws would be necessary. Their initial lists showed that each group was well able to understand the need for laws to protect their own interests and that of the community as a whole. The farmers and fishermen decided that:

- Our land and our waters must not be polluted.

- Everyone should be able to vote, including people made slaves as a punishment.

- There should be a reasonable price for our meat, fish and crops.

Scribes decided:

- The government should be made up of scribes and nobles.

- Everyone should be allowed to go to school – rich and poor.

- We should be paid for as much as we teach but we must teach the poor kids too.

The children were then re-grouped so that each new group contained one person from each of the initial interest groups. Each new group then had to come up with laws with which all would agree. This invoked heated discussion but the end results provided evidence that the children were able to compromise and to select the 'fairest' rules. One group decided:

1   Nobles, craftsmen and farmers should all be in the parliament.

2   Everyone should get at least 1 shekel a week to keep them going because if they can't get jobs for some reason they won't be able to buy food.

3   If you murder someone you should get murdered in the same way: it is only fair that if you take someone's life, yours gets taken.

4   Everyone over 14 except foreign slaves should be allowed to vote (because people didn't live so long and so 14 would be considered quite old).

5   Polluting the waters is illegal because it will damage fish, farms and people.

6   Everyone should respect one another, because if they don't, people's communities will fall apart.

7   Everyone that earns money should pay 30% of their profits towards taxes.

8   If you nick the farmers' crops or livestock you will be starved for 3 days.

9   If you steal you will have your hand cut off to prevent you from doing it again.

While some of these laws may appear harsh, they do show a concern for justice. Some were surprisingly close to those in the Code of Hammurabi, for example:

- If a man puts out the eye of another man he shall have his own eye put out.

Other laws from the Code provide for fruitful discussion, for example:

- If a doctor makes a large incision and cures the person he shall receive 10 shekels. If he saves the life of a slave, he shall receive 2 shekels.

- If a fire breaks out in a house and someone who comes to put out the fire takes some of the property, he shall be thrown on that fire.

The class were fascinated by these early laws and went on to discuss these in great depth, along with the rules in their school and the laws of the U.K., illustrating the ability of children of 9–11 to engage with aspects of political literacy.

*With thanks to the children of
Sandford School, Crediton, Devon.*

The Global Dimension of Citizenship Education

7

In creating citizenship and human rights education we also create optimism, because worst of all are the cynics around us who believe nothing can be done . . . who destroy people's belief that we can really change the world around us. (Blunkett, 1999)

Is it fair that we get big beds to lie on
And they get a small blanket?
Is it fair that we have a good education
And they get none?
Is it fair that we get proper meals
And they get small scraps?
Is it fair for them?
Is it fair for us?
(Poem by 9-year-old boy 2000)

Introduction

Introducing a global dimension into the curriculum means more than studying the activities of people in places beyond our own locality. It involves learning about the relationships between ourselves and others. In this way global education can be typified as a social, cultural and moral pursuit through which the learner evaluates her/his own position and actions in the world.

Key issues

Building empathy and understanding

How can we foster understanding and sensitivity for the feelings and needs of others in the world, particularly those who live in different material conditions? How can we foster respect for the achievements of others? How can we foster a sense of common humanity, of common needs and rights? How can we prepare our students to establish successful links with children living in different locations in the world?

Globalisation and the exchange of goods and culture

How can we help students explore issues of justice and fairness in our global communications systems and the exchange of goods around the world? How can we communicate the complexity of global relationships and their historical antecedents? How can we expand the horizons of children who live in less diverse communities?

Promoting active global citizenship

How can we support students in developing confidence that their actions can make a difference? How can we build their optimism and maintain their morale in hoping and working for a safer and fairer world? How can they learn about power relationships? How can they learn about contributing towards sustainable development?

Findings from research

Building empathy and understanding

The theme 'getting on with others' has been central to global education at least since the early 1980s, when the Schools' Council first launched the World Studies 8–13 Project. The process of understanding self and self with others is implicit in this focus, an interplay between 'ego' and 'alter' which is fundamental to the socialisation of self within a plural society (Davies and Rey 1998). The well-publicised Early Years Reggio Emilia programme aims to ensure that new generations will not accept fascism and prioritises this kind of intercultural process. Activities are designed to enable young learners to 'see self again' through a multiplicity of perspectives (Fawcett and Duckett 2000). Parekh also emphasises the importance of such mutuality to the development of shared understandings across cultural and material boundaries:

> To be in a conversation means to be beyond oneself, to think with the other and to come back to oneself as another. (Parekh 2000: 337)

At the same time concern has been expressed about continuing Anglo/Eurocentric bias in curricula (Gundara 2000) in England and in other European countries. Said issues a challenge to educators:

> Without significant exception the universalising discourses of modern Europe and the United States assume the silence, willing or otherwise, of the non-European world. ... There is only infrequently an acknowledgement that the colonised people should be heard from, their ideas known. (Said 1993: 581)

Research with young people in school has indicated that their understanding reflects such narrow views of others in the wider world and that their main source of information is television (Midwinter 1994). The process of establishing direct links through which students gain access to the voices of children living in different material and cultural conditions can counter the effects of such Eurocentrism by promoting new understandings and empathetic relationships (Tanner 1998, Anderson 1998).

Globalisation and the exchange of goods and culture

That we live in 'global age' is in part evidenced by the rapid exchange of goods and services through worldwide web sites which provide access to and information about music, art and a full range of community ventures. Thus we may turn to http://perso.wanadoo.fr/willmenter/ to learn about a musician from the U.K. making sound sculptures in France or to www.bham.net/soe/stm/ to read about musicians playing the Zimbabwean mbira in the U.K. Another source of information about globalisation and the exchange of goods is the growing number of web sites advertising tourism in 'less economically developed countries'.

Reports on projects undertaken in schools by artists with knowledge and skills of different art forms from different parts of the world indicate that students are receptive to and appreciative of difference (Kushner 1991). These exchanges can inspire the learner to recognise the value given to their own ideas as they are incorporated into a new product for performance (Clough and Tarr 2000).

Promoting active global citizenship

This aim lies at the heart of the strategy being developed by the U.K. Department for International Development. They are committed to 'working for increased public understanding of global interdependence and the need for international development . . . [and] to achieve attitude change across society' (Short 1999). Research by Hicks and Holden indicates that between the ages of 11 and 14 students at school become increasingly pessimistic about the prospect of alleviating poverty, hardship and pollution worldwide (Hicks and Holden 1995). This tension between hopelessness and hopefulness is echoed in research about global relationships. Bauman argues that 'the links between privileged and under-privileged are now fractured in an increasingly polarised world', and he questions the possibility of effecting change for increased social justice (Bauman 1998:88). Beck on the other hand argues that no-one knows whether social justice is possible in the global age but to fail to rise to the challenge is the greatest risk for democracy. He recommends that amongst other measures we should 'strengthen social networks of self-provision and self-organisation and raise and keep alive world issues of social and economic justice in the centres of global civil society' (Beck 2001:155). Thus in preparing students to be globally active citizens we need a programme of intercultural learning with these aims:

- overcoming ethnocentrism through developing consciousness that one's perception is influenced by culture and experience

- acquiring the ability to empathise with other cultures through developing an openness towards the unfamiliar and unknown

- acquiring the ability to communicate across cultural boundaries

- developing a means of co-operation across cultural boundaries in a multicultural setting.

(Fennes and Hapgood 1997: 44)

113

Activities

Exploring perceptions through photographs:
'Most likely to . . .?'

Purpose

- To explore and challenge preconceptions and stereotypes (G, CE)

- To encourage observation, questioning, discussion/speaking (CE)

- To enable students to share what they already know (G)

- To develop students' thinking skills (G, CE)

Preparation

You will need:

- good quality photographs of children (one from a Less Economically Developed Country (LEDC) and one from a More Economically Developed Country (MEDC)

- most likely to . . . statement sheet (Handout 22).

Procedures

Students work in groups of three. They discuss each statement and decide which is most likely to belong to which photograph. They put the statement number in the correct side of the sheet. Students must be able to justify their decision. Each group of three then joins with another group to form a six: they compare and discuss their decisions. Students who finish before the rest can then make up further statements. Bring the whole class together for a final discussion, and focus on between three and four statements. This is a chance for you and the students to challenge misconceptions or at least recognise that there may be alternative views and justifications.

Plenary

- How did you make decisions?
- What reasoning/evidence have you to support this decision?
- How did you resolve disagreements?
- How useful/accurate are the photographs as a source of evidence?
- What issues cropped up in your discussions?
- What did you learn about how we stereotype?
- What thinking did you do? Can these skills be used in other situations?

Possibilities

'Most likely to . . .' can be easily adapted to other themes and concepts, for example:

- Employment structures – primary, secondary and tertiary industry;
- Urban zones – inner city and outer suburbs;
- Regional contrasts – north and south Italy, Amazonia, S.E and N.E. Brazil.

All these could be based around photographs, diagrams or just words.

Note: This activity is particularly useful at the beginning of a topic as it enables you to assess what the students already know (or think they know). It is accessible to all students and particularly to those who may feel more confident to contribute orally. It can last 10 minutes or a whole lesson; you can use five statements or twenty statements.

With thanks to Rachel Bennet, Cullompton Community College.

115

Decide whether it is Mputo or Sarah who is most likely to . . .

Most likely to . . .	Mputo because . . .	Sarah because . . .
1 . . . help their parents with the chores?		
2 . . . have a bicycle?		
3 . . . enjoy school?		
4 . . . like singing and being told stories?		
5 . . . feel loved?		
6 . . . have most friends?		
7 . . . steal from a shop?		
8 . . . get headaches?		
9 . . . have a faith (religion)?		
10 . . . get a smack for being naughty?		
11 . . . get spoiled by grandparents?		
12 . . . be happy with their life?		

Possibilities plus

Questioning a photograph

Organise children in groups. Give out a large sheet of paper to each table and place a photograph in the centre of each sheet. Explain to the children that they must look at the photograph closely and write clearly in the space around the photograph any questions they would like to ask and any statements they know 'for sure' about the photographs. After five minutes pass the sheet and photograph to the next table, with that table passing theirs on so that all photographs and sheets are moved round in a clockwise direction. When a group receives a photograph and sheet, they should look at what the previous group has written and see if they can answer any of their questions and then add some statements and questions of their own. This process continues until all children have seen all five or six photographs and the photographs are back with the original groups. Then give out the information about the photographs or about the locality in general. It is important that each group, having digested the information, shares this with the rest of the class so that they all learn about the activities or people in the specific photograph. The plenary should focus on what they have learnt from each other, what misconceptions they had and what more they would like to know.

Extending a photo: what's the rest of the story?

Children work in small groups to think what lies beyond the photograph. Each group has a photograph placed in the centre of a large sheet of paper and they must then draw what is beyond the scene in front of them, thus extending the photograph. This requires the children to think about what kind of buildings or vegetation would lie beyond the photograph and draw on their knowledge of the local environment. Discussion can focus on how they made decisions and what more they need to know.

Put yourself in the picture

Give each pair of children a photograph. Give each child a post-it with a smiley face drawn on it. After discussing the photograph in pairs, they then decide where they would like to be in the picture and place the smiley face accordingly. Ask the children to close their eyes and consider what it is like to be in the picture. What does it smell like? Look like? Sound like? What questions would they like to ask the other people in the photo?

Global marketplace: the chocolate trade

Purpose

- To help students understand the history and significance of the chocolate trade (G)

- To help students consider relationships between the producer, the consumer and the trader with reference to the chocolate trade (G, CE)

- To relate this to issues of power and justice (CE)

- To provide opportunities for art and design (Art, D & T)

Preparation

You will need:

- materials about chocolate production available from Cadbury's

- wrappers from commercially produced chocolate products, including Fair Trade

- historical source material about Cortes and the Aztecs

Procedure

Children use different sources of information to research the following areas:

- The history of chocolate drinking and production

- The process of farming cacao beans

- The work of those involved (and the pay received)

- The fairness of relationships between the producer, the trader and the consumer.

Plenary

Each group should share their results and discuss:

- What are the main differences between the ways in which the cacao bean was used by the Aztecs and the ways in which we use it today?

- What do the farmers, the transporters, the traders and the customers think about the chocolate trade? How does it affect each group?

- How much of your own money have you spent on chocolate in your life?

- How much of the total has gone to the actual farmers of the cacao bean?

Possibilities

As a follow-up, children can be asked to design a Fair Trade chocolate bar which is attractive to children. To advertise their bar, they will need to think about how to explain to others the issues of economics and social justice behind Fair Trade. They must also think of the features of good design and what makes people respond to advertisements. They need to design packaging, think of a brand name and create a slogan or catch phrase.

This fits in well with work in history on the Aztecs. There are also links with science, including the source of chocolate and the implications of eating chocolate for health and diet. It could be part of a project on food and trade, looking at, for example, the banana trade or the coffee trade. This could include discussion of child labour and cash crops. It is important for students to know that there are groups working to protect the rights of workers so materials from such organisations are essential.

The traditions and travels of reggae music

Purpose

*   To provide information about the origins and significance of reggae music in Jamaica (Mus)
*   To provide information about the spread of reggae music and the significance of reggae lyrics on the African continent (Mus, H, G)
*   To acknowledge the interdependence of musicians (CE)
*   To enjoy music from different cultural settings (CE)

Preparation

You will need copies of Handout 23 (one per group) and copies of a world map. You can draw on the texts *The Rough Guide to World Music* (Broughton *et al.* 1994), *People Funny Boy: the Genius of Lee 'Scratch' Perry* (Katz 2000) and www.ritchie-hardin.com/reggae, to provide further information.

Procedure

Whole class session: play some reggae music and show pictures down loaded from the above website. In groups students then study the words of two of Bob Marley's songs: e.g. 'Songs of Freedom' and 'Stand Up for Your Rights' and decide which they think is the best song and why. Students then sort the information cards (see below) on to a timeline so as to present 'the story of reggae'. They record the movement of reggae on their world maps. In their groups they discuss:

*   What are the origins of reggae music?
*   Why is reggae sometimes called music of resistance?
*   What do you know about Bob Marley and his life?
*   What events have been celebrated by reggae music?
*   How has the spirit of reggae music been created again and again?
*   How has reggae music spread around the world?
*   How do musicians around the world learn from each other?

Plenary

Students present their timelines and shared answers to the above questions. They can discuss their favourite reggae song as a stimulus to bringing in recordings of other reggae songs that they have access to.

Possibilities

Students could research other forms of reggae music that can be heard in their own region. For example these bands and musics can be heard in the southwest of England: Wild Bunch (with Tricky) (Dub, 1990s), Roni Size (Jungle, live shows, 1990s–2000s), Massive Attack (Hip Hop, live 1990s–2000s), House and Garage styles which sample original Bob Marley lyrics, Asian Dub Foundation (late 1990s–2000s). Students can then discuss why reggae music has remained popular and how it might continue as a political movement or a youth-cultural movement.

With thanks to Ben Clough.

Marcus Garvey campaigned in the 1920s and 1930s for black unity. He encouraged his followers to dream of a return to Africa.	When slavery was abolished in 1838 the British had to find other ways of working the plantations. They brought in new workers from Angola.	Bob Marley sang for freedom and wanted people to remember what Marcus Garvey had said. He lived from 1945–1981. His last song was 'Songs of Freedom'. He died young from cancer.
In the early 1960s a music called Ska developed, played on piano, electric guitar, drums and brass instruments. The Skatalites still play today.	Lee Scratch Perry was a famous music star from the 1950s to 1970s. He worked with The Wailers and became famous for his production of dub music	The Ethiopian Emperor Hailie Selassie visited Jamaica in 1968. After this Reggae became popular in Kingston, Jamaica.
Reggae bands in the 1970s included Burning Spear, Toots and the Maytals, The Wailers. Marley became a symbol of rebellion all over the world through his music with the Wailers.	Marley's most famous concerts were the 'One Love' Concert in 1978 and a concert to celebrate Zimbabwean Independence in 1980. Both of these celebrated the end of conflicts.	Reggae is a popular music in many African countries. Lucky Dube from South Africa (1984 onwards) and Alpha Blondy from the Ivory Coast are two of the most famous African reggae stars.
By 1670 when the Spanish lost control of Jamaica to the British, the majority of the population were African slaves mostly from Ghana.	The Angolan workers made sure that they kept their culture and gave themselves the name 'Bongo Nation'.	The Maroons developed their own percussion music. Later on this inspired Reggae musicians.
Rastafarians are a small but important religious group in Jamaica. Rasta music is played at ceremonies called nyabingis. Many reggae musicians have been Rastafarians.	When the British arrived after defeating the Spanish many slaves fled to the hills. They lived in the hills and were later called 'Maroons'.	The folk traditions of the Jamaican peoples drew on the culture of the Maroons and Bongo Nation (Angolans).

Tourism: do we want the new hotel?

Purpose

- To help students consider the advantages and disadvantages of tourism (G, CE)

- To explore the conflicting interests involved in development and change (G, CE)

- To add to students' knowledge of the geography of Kenya (G)

- To encourage students to consider their own role as a consumer of tourism (CE)

- To introduce issues of sustainability and planning for the future (Sci, CE)

Preparation

You will need:

- the information sheet (Handout 24) about a new hotel to be built in Mombasa, an island connected by road and rail to the mainland of Kenya.

- writing frames for each group (below)

- a map of Mombasa, showing its proximity to the mainland and tourist areas (Tsavo national park, Shimba Hills animal reserve, the coast)

- tourist brochures promoting Kenya

Procedure

Whole class initial discussion: What is tourism? Who has been a tourist? Where did they go? What parts of Britain attract tourists? What parts of the world attract tourists? Why? What are the benefits and disadvantages of tourism to a country?

Now introduce Kenya as a country which relies heavily on tourism for its income, illustrating this with tourist brochures. Then introduce the island of Mombasa, Kenya, where a new hotel is to be built. Have a brief discussion focusing on:

- What will tourists want to do if they come to this hotel?

- Who might benefit from the new hotel?

- Who might lose out?

Give out the background information sheet and divide the class into eight groups, giving each group a writing frame. Explain that they must not only consider their own case but also the concerns of one or two of the other groups. After completing the writing frames, each group reads out its case and the case for one other group. Then hold a discussion:

- Which groups had strong arguments? Why?

- In what ways were the interests of others considered?

- Who has the most power to influence the development of the site?

- Whose interests should Kenya consider when planning for the future?

- What other countries have similar dilemmas?

- What responsibilities do we have as tourists?

Possibilities

This could be extended into a debate instead of students reading out their written work. Each group could have 3 minutes to present its case, based on the arguments in their writing frames.

Writing frames

Each group should have a writing frame with information specific to their group and then the common format, beginning 'we would like to argue that . . .' (see group I, Handout 25, for an example).

Group 2

You represent the local people in the building trade. You want the hotel to be built. Why? What good will come from the building of the hotel?

Group 3

You represent the Islamic community. You do not want the hotel to be built. Why? Think of how it will affect your lives generally. Try to think also of what good might come from the hotel being built.

Group 4

You represent the Kenyan National Tourist Office. You want the hotel to be built. Why? Think of what the hotel would mean to this part of Kenya as a whole.

Group 5

You represent the conservationists concerned to preserve the ecology of the coral reef. You do not want the hotel to be built. Why?

Group 6

You represent the local transport police. The hotel will be built near a major road, causing short-term disruption to traffic. You do not want the hotel to be built. Why?

Group 7

You represent the owners of the market stalls that use the land where the planned hotel is to be built. You do not want the hotel to be built. Why? Think of how it will affect your life generally.

Group 8

You represent the local unemployed poor people. You are finding it hard to survive. Each day is a case of looking for your next meal. You want the hotel to be built. Why?

123

HANDOUT 24

The proposal for building the Swahili Hotel: information sheet

The hotel is to be built on land that is used regularly by market stall-holders in Mombasa.

The site is close to the beach, which is very popular with tourists.

It is a busy area with shops and craftspeople to be seen everywhere you go.

There is an Islamic mosque (place of worship for Muslims) situated very close to the site.

The hotel would be built very close to a major road, causing traffic diversions and disruption.

The Shimba Hills Animal Reserve and the Tsavo National Park are only a short distance away and very popular with tourists.

There is a coral reef running the length of the Kenyan coast. Conservationists are worried about further damage to this natural resource from pleasure boats, divers and other tourist activities.

One in six people in the area are unemployed and there is a high crime rate.

Additional Information

Tourism is the world's fastest growing industry. In 1950 25 million people travelled abroad, in 1999 it was 670 million. The World Tourism Organisation estimates that by 2020 some 1.6 billion people will travel each year. The growth area is long haul travel, especially to developing countries.

Water shortage will be an increasing problem: WWF has calculated that a tourist in Spain uses 880 litres of water per day, compared with 250 litres by a local.

By 2025, the number of people living in areas where renewable water is scarce will increase from 130 million to more than 1 billion.

(The Guardian, 12 May 2001)

Group 1

You represent the Swahili Hotel Corporation. You are responsible for putting forward the proposal for building the hotel. You want the hotel to be built. Why? What are the advantages of building a hotel in this location, not just for you but for the local community?

We would like to argue that . . . .

We understand that it will be difficult for . . . .

Therefore we feel that it would be in the best interest of these groups to

Case study: do we want the new hotel?

Owners of market stalls

We would like to argue that if you are going to build your hotel then all our sheds that store our meat and fish and vegetables and the rest of our things would be knocked down and to build them will cost more money. So why can't the hotel move? Or people that are employed are going to be unemployed.

We understand that it will be difficult for the Muslims because the place where they pray would be more noisy. And it will make lots of road works so the transport police won't like it.

Therefore we feel that it would be in the best interest of these groups not to have a hotel there.

Kenyan National Tourist Office

We would like to argue that it would be a good idea because it would attract tourists and lots of money. It will get the homeless off the streets and let them have a job. It is a good idea because it is near the sea and near the animal parks and it is near the airport so the tourists won't have to travel far to the hotel.

We understand it will be difficult for the market stall owners because they would have to move, but they would have more customers so it wouldn't matter too much.

Therefore we feel it would be in the best interest of these groups to build the hotel because we would make more jobs and more money from the tourists and the safari parks would make more money.

Upottery Primary School, Year 4/5
Adapted from an idea by Michael Whiting
Student, Exeter University.

The energy debate

Purpose

- To provide information about the many ways of generating power (Sci)

- To help students articulate arguments about the application of science (Sci, CE)

- To help students understand that methods of obtaining energy are controversial and that there are no 'right' answers (Sci, CE)

- To help students understand the global dimension to the energy debate (Sci, CE)

Preparation

Students should have done some prior work on different sources of power and energy conservation: e.g. fossil fuels, hydroelectric, nuclear, geothermal, solar and wind powered electricity. You will need:

- reference materials including web sites, promotional material, videos.

- photos of the power sources in the centre of large sheets of sugar paper with a central line dividing the page into two: one side headed 'for' and the other 'against'.

Procedure

Session 1

Explain that they are going to have a filmed debate about which is the best energy source for the future. You may wish to discuss what 'best' is and offer a

range of definitions. Arrange the students in mixed ability groups of five or six and allocate a power source to each group. Prompt the students to come up with as many arguments for and against their source as they can. Remind them that they will not only have to give a good argument in its favour but also defend it against others' criticisms. Allow some time for this and help them access source material.

Ask each group to come up with a question or criticism of the other sources and list these on the board. The groups will want further time to prepare answers to these new attacks. Keep a copy of these questions and allocate them to individuals to raise in the debate; more questions can be added later if required. Now ask them to produce visual aids to make their case stronger. Each member of the group should take a part in the process and practise their part. One member should be voted as spokesperson for the group to field questions.

Session 2

Arrange a semi-circle of tables in a large space such as a hall with seating for each group. Appoint a chair person (or take the job yourself) to lead the debate. Appoint a reporter and camera person to minute and film the debate. Outline a clear programme for the debate such as:

*   Introduction of groups

*   3 minutes per group to make the case for their own energy source.

*   Tabled questions to be asked of each group in turn with time allowed for answers from the representatives.

*   An open session to allow extra questioning and answers that have arisen during the debate.

Plenary

After the debate, hold a discussion:

*   How did it feel having to defend your particular energy source?

*   Were you persuaded by others' arguments? Why or why not?

*   Which source of energy is most expensive? Why?

*   Which sources of energy have negative effects, e.g. cause pollution?

*   Which sources of energy affect people in other countries?

*   How can we conserve energy?

You may want to ask for a show of hands or open a discussion on how best to choose the energy source for the future.

Possibilities

If it has been possible to make a video recording of the debate, watching it and discussing the success of the debate in terms of their skill at asking and answering questions is very rewarding. With secondary students this work could be developed so that students consider power sources in different countries, thus introducing a global dimension. This could relate to debates about ecological influences, renewable resources and global responsibilities with regard to the use of energy. For all students visits to power stations, wind farms etc. are invaluable. For primary children, this work can be extended in Design Technology where they can make working models using water, wind and solar power.

Case study: the energy debate – work in and out of the classroom

I used this debate to link our work in Science with a global perspective and citizenship. The children had quite firm preferences at the start of the topic and there was some resistance to adopting and arguing for the obviously 'unpopular' options. We discussed this and emphasised that exploring all the energy sources equally was important as in their role as scientists they needed to be able to make informed decisions. In the end those with a source of energy that was 'difficult' to promote or defend were the best prepared.

We followed up this work with a residential trip to North Wales. We visited a decommissioned nuclear power station, where the children were able to put their questioning skills to the test: they asked why Greenpeace objected to the outfall from Sellafield and heard the representative argue that there were also objections to wind farms. We had visited an anti-wind farm website earlier to understand the nature of their protest and had visited the Greenpeace website to find out about their support. The children were thus able to look at the various arguments, considering all points of view. While in North Wales we also visited a hydro-electric power station and the Centre for Alternative Technology where the children began to understand how different power sources are useful in different circumstances: a useful lead into the use of energy in different parts of the world.

*With thanks to Beth Gompertz,
Inverteign Primary School.*

Europe and the environment: countries without borders

Purpose

- To help students understand the political map of Europe (G)

- To help students understand that economic activity in one country affects the environment of another (CE, G, Sci)

- To increase the knowledge base of students about specific environmental risks within European borders (CE, Sci)

- To understand the role of pan European co-operation and legislation in matters of the environment (CE)

Preparation

You will need resources and information on one or more of the following:

1   Acid rain (origins and effects of sulphur emissions)

2   The accident in 1986 in a chemical factory near Basle, Switzerland which polluted the river Rhine through different countries and into the North Sea

3   Chernobyl

4   The outbreak of foot and mouth in 2001

A good starting point is the internet, (for example www.planet.com). You will also need: a political map of Europe, copies of this for students' use and coloured pencils.

Procedure

Whole class:

Briefly introduce the problems associated with each of these cases, including key background information.

Groupwork:

The students research their chosen topic from the different sources of information. They should consider the following questions:

- What was the cause of this disaster?
- What happened?
- Where were the effects felt?
- Which communities suffered?
- What was done to resolve the problems?

Students should plot the course of the events on their maps. Each group should agree a short statement about the need for local, national and European policies to solve the problems caused. These statements are read out and/or put on display.

Plenary

- How does environmental activity in one country affect another?
- How did countries co-operate to try and resolve the problems?
- What more should governments do?
- Are political borders important? What for?
- What does it mean: 'we share a common environment'?

Possibilities

Students can do further research related to the effects of acid rain. They can investigate 'Europe's sulphur budget', looking at the balance of sulphur emissions and depositions. On their maps of Europe they can indicate with coloured pencils those countries which emit more sulphur than is deposited in them, and in a different colour indicate those that receive more pollution that they emit. Sweden is a good example: they can note all the countries that contribute to the pollution of Swedish forests and lakes.

With thanks to Carmen Gonzalo and Maria Villanueva, Universitat Autonoma de Barcelona.

Demba's life: what's it really like?

Purpose

- To appreciate and respect different lifestyles (G, CE)
- To understand how physical and human geography influence people's quality of life (G)
- To develop listening, recall memory and extended writing skills (E, CE)
- To help students appreciate how stories can change in the telling and the implications of this (CE)
- To learn some of the geography of Mali (G)

Preparation

You will need:

- the story (Handout 26)
- a resource sheet
- a story board or writing frame where necessary

Procedures

Divide the students into three groups: A, B, C. Send out those in groups B and C with a classroom assistant to do a pre-set task. Tell group A that they are going to have to retell the story to the others. Students should not write anything – just close their eyes, listen, relax and concentrate. After you have read the story allow them to ask a couple of questions to clarify information. Some students may find a resource sheet helpful to jot down reminders for when they retell the story. Group B then comes back and is told the story by group A. Group C then returns and is told the story by Group B. Group A should listen out for any inaccuracies or omissions from their original version. Students then compare and contrast their versions, noting any observations. Finish with a whole class discussion with groups feeding back to establish what was remembered and what they have learned.

If you are not able to send out two groups, this activity can also be done very effectively as a whole class. Read the story to the students and then give them 10–15 minutes to write up the story as they remember it. Ask them not to discuss it with anyone else. Ask students some questions (see plenary) and then let them compare and contrast their stories in pairs and then perhaps in groups of four. Bring the whole class back together and draw out the main teaching points.

Plenary

• What was the first thing you remembered?

• What did you remember after some thought?

• What type of things were most important to remember? Why?

• What things are least important to remember? Why?

• What strategies can we use to remember things?

• Are there occasions when stories are re-told and changed in the telling?

• What can be the consequences of this?

• How can we know when people are telling the truth?

• What did you learn about Mali?

• What did you learn about Demba's life? What problems does he face?

• What are these caused by? What solutions might there be?

Possibilities

You can use stories in texts or newspapers or you can make up a story based on researched information. Story telling needs to involve characters and be personal to make it real. It can be used in many subjects. Other ideas which link geography and citizenship are:

• A personal account of a natural hazard, e.g. Indian earthquake, Bangladesh cyclone, Nevada del Ruiz volcanic eruption

• A personal account of somebody migrating, e.g. from South to North Italy, from Mexico to USA

• A personal account of a Kayapoo tribesman.

History teachers can use eye-witness accounts of key events, extracts from journals or newspapers, extracts from historical novels. The emphasis should be on learning historical information at the same time as developing the skills taught in citizenship education: participation, enquiry and communication.

Follow-up sessions

In the next lesson students could be asked to classify and categorise information they can remember from the story (no more than ten words in each section of the board). They need to think about what information to include and what to leave out in order to produce a good piece of geographical writing. At this point you might need to re-read the story. For homework they can draft a newspaper article retelling Demba's story remembering what was discussed in the lesson. Some students may benefit from a word bank.

Demba's story and 'Most likely to' both come from a Year 9 scheme of work which links citizenship with a geography unit on World Development, devised by Rachel Bennett, Cullompton Community College. The activities were developed as part of a Thinking Skills Project, which was part of 'On the Line 2000'. This was set up to celebrate the millennium and help students learn about the eight countries on the Greenwich Meridian. More information on the Thinking Skills Project can be found on www.devon.gov.uk/dcs/geog/line/repo1/index.html, including the complete scheme of work for Year 9 on World Development. The activity in Chapter 5 'Why is Ranjesh's mother crying?' was also devised for the Thinking Skills project. The two teachers involved talk about their work on page 135.

Demba's story

Bonjour, my name is **Demba**.

I live in **Mali** with my uncle, aunt and my **three** girl cousins. The name of my village is **Tomora,** which is in the **Sahel region of Africa.** We live near the **River Niger.** The climate is very **hot** and **dry.** Sometimes the temperature reaches **40°C.** Most of the year it is dry, but the rains do come around **July to September** although sometimes they are late or there is not enough, so we get a **drought.** Where I live there are only small bushes and trees. My uncle remembers when there used to be more vegetation here, but the soil is becoming **infertile** because farmers are putting too many animals in their fields and not leaving their fields **fallow** for a while. We all live together in our hut which is made of wood with a grass thatched roof. I helped my uncle build it. It needs to be repaired now, but it is hard to find wood for building and repairing homes and cooking because so many people have **cut down the trees.** Sometimes my aunt has to walk miles to find fuel – it is becoming a real problem. I can speak **French** but I prefer to talk in **Bambara.** I wake up at **5.30 am** and eat and then go to the fields. I go to bed about **8 pm.** I meet my friends on the way home from the fields and we play, sing and dance. In the fields I help my uncle weed, **irrigate** the land, sow and harvest – there is always something to do. Often in the heat of the day we rest under a tree. My cousins help my aunt do the housework, cooking, cleaning, collecting firewood and water from the village **well.** They carry the water in buckets on their heads. Some of the water is used for domestic needs and some for watering our small vegetable plot. We are never sure where the next year's supply of food will come from. There have been below average harvests for the past **3 years** but there is not a crisis yet! We grow **millet** as there is little rain in Tomora. This is our staple food. My uncle has two small fields which we work by hand using hoes. We can usually grow enough food to last **4–6 months.** My uncle used to have **oxen and goats,** but we had to sell them during the dry years when we could not grow enough food. After the harvest last **November,** we all moved to find food and earn money. My aunt moved with the girls to her cousins by the River Niger and worked **threshing rice.** What she earned was used to pay the family tax bill. My uncle went to **Toguere,** which is a market town. He found casual work as a **brick layer.** What he earned was used to buy extra onions, salt and fish. As for me, I went **south** to find work in the **market gardens,** but I wasn't able to bring any extra cash home with me. By **March** we were all back in Tomora to work the fields. It is a really hard time before the harvests, we are down to **one meal a day.** Everyone works long hours in the hot season. My aunt had another baby girl and could not go out to look for wild foods to improve our diet. I had to leave the fields to go and collect wild grains. This year we were lucky. My younger uncle has sent money from the **Ivory Coast** where he went to find work. Now we can buy millet. If it lasts until the harvest, and the rains are good, perhaps we will be able to buy a goat! My uncle wants to start to grow **cash crops,** like **groundnuts** to make more money, but I'm not sure that is a good idea else what will we eat? He says we can get money from the Government if we stop growing our own food.

Case study: teachers talking about thinking skills

What are the benefits of teaching thinking skills?

The actual thinking skills themselves have been enormously beneficial in terms of getting the children to communicate with each other and also with you in that they tend to want to ask you questions rather than you constantly asking them questions. So it creates a lot of dialogue between teacher and pupil which is useful because then you can find out their understanding and their knowledge. It has developed my teaching, made me think really carefully about how I question children, be more open ended, and push their thinking forward.

It gives children the confidence to speak out or to write down their thoughts, because they know that you're not going to say 'That's wrong'. Instead it's: 'Why do you think that?' 'How can you justify that?' 'Has anyone got an alternative?' 'OK, which do we think is the best way?' Lots of staff won't like to do it because technically it looks like you've got no control, but the control is different in that they are working and controlling themselves: you're not standing up at the front giving them the right answer. We've found that the low ability kids who might have problems sitting down and working with a text book think they are just having a nice time, but actually when you re-cap on what learning they have acquired, it's huge. They feel positive because, if you like, in Maths they're pressured to give the right answer, whereas in Geography and R.E., as long as they have learned to be able to justify, they feel secure in their own ability to be able to stand up and say 'Hey, what about this?' And often they come up with things that we wouldn't have even thought of.

How does teaching thinking skills help relate citizenship to geography and R.E.?

For R.E., it leads into questioning their own individuality which links to citizenship, and expressing their own points of view and opinions whilst ensuring that they are becoming more aware of cultures and religions. From a geographical point of view, obviously there are links between citizenship and different cultures and lifestyles. We were looking at cocao farmers in Ghana. We used a video and compared different lifestyles and looked at issues like Oxfam, Fair Trade products, etc., which links the concept of trade to geography and to citizenship. Also what we've found from doing this particular project is a link between geography and R.E. because one of the things about thinking skills is how can you transfer these skills not only from one subject to another, but from one context to another, from school to home, in their own lives, etc.

What happens if students come up with values or statements that you think are not acceptable?

There are ways of questioning and talking around those, and you have to say 'OK, that is one point of view, however what do you think maybe a Christian would say about that?' You have to be aware that some kids may deliberately come up with something that is controversial and you just have to be prepared to deal with it. Very often before I can say 'Well yes, that is one point of view, have you thought about . . .' other kids will say 'You can't say that!' They will listen to their peers more than you, so if other children are saying 'How can you say that when blah, blah, blah . . .' that is probably more valuable than me questioning them. I had a student saying that they don't have shops, and everyone just turned around and looked at this child and said: 'Course they do!' Then they say 'Well why did you think that?' and the discussion carries on: 'Oh, cause on telly all you ever see is . . .'.

What you have to be prepared for is to deviate from your lesson plan and engage in dialogue and talk and go with the flow, but also you have to have the skill to stop it when it's appropriate. It's hard saying 'talk about this, do it in pairs' then getting them back, then off again, then back again. You've got to have very strong classroom rules, like respecting what everybody says, with no-one laughing at anyone. You've got to be a good, confident teacher.

Rachel Bennett (Geography) and Sarah Leslie (R.E.)
from Cullompton Community College were talking to Cathie Holden.

Activity for staff discussion

Where do we draw the line?

Purpose

- To promote discussion among staff about what actions are acceptable as part of education for citizenship

- To help staff reach consensus about school policy

Preparation

You will need:

- a set of statements (see page 137), cut up, for each pair of participants (each set should be on a different colour of card or labelled set A, set B etc.)

- a piece of string (to represent a continuum) laid out on a table top. Label one end of the continuum 'acceptable' and the other 'unacceptable'.

Procedure

Give each pair of participants a set of the statements. Ask them to discuss and then place each card in turn at an agreed point along the continuum. Then explain that having placed their cards they must decide (as a pair) where to 'draw the line'. In other words they must decide at which point on the continuum they will put an X to indicate that all actions to the left are acceptable, and those to the right are unacceptable. (Participants can use a slip of paper in the same colour as their set of cards to do this, or put their initials on a slip of paper and use this.)

Then bring together the whole group and discuss where people 'drew the line' and why, and which statements caused the most dissension or discussion. Ask pairs to justify/defend their decisions.

Plenary

- Which of these actions would you consider to be part of education for citizenship? Why? Why not?

- Which should we encourage?

- What are the implications for school policy?

Adapted from an idea by Graham Pike and David Selby (originally published in Earthkind – see resources).

Statements for discussion

1 Children decide to take action in support of animal rights, after a class discussion.

2 Staff take a decision not to have a vending machine selling drinks and snacks.

3 After a racist incident, a teacher explains to the class why she finds this unacceptable.

4 After learning about child labour in a geography lesson, students arrange a boycott of some local shops. They want to encourage others to join in.

5 The local town council asks for a group of students to be released from school to attend a meeting on developing a piece of wasteland for leisure activities.

6 Students learn about the activities of a number of organisations working for change, including Greenpeace and Amnesty International.

7 After a lesson on justice and the law, students decide to write to their local MP on school headed paper about legalising cannabis.

8 The head teacher instructs children to collect rubbish from the playground during lunchbreaks.

9 A teacher works with his students to discard school books which misrepresent minority groups.

10 As part of a local study a teacher encourages children to learn more about why a new group of refugees has moved to the area and how they might be helped.

11 Through the School Council, students ask for more choice in the curriculum and request that there is no school uniform.

12 Students discuss the pros and cons of nuclear power in Science and ask the teacher for her views. She gives these, along with her reasons for holding them.

References

Anderson, B. (1991) *Imagined Communities*, London: Verso.

Anderson, G. (1998) 'Children's Newspapers: Meeting Other Minds', in C. Holden and N. Clough (eds) *Children as Citizens: Education for Participation*, London: Jessica Kingsley.

Arnot, M., Gray, J., James, M. and Rudduck, J. (1998) *Recent Research on Gender and Educational Performance*, Ofsted.

Ascherson, N. in *The Observer* 27/9/98.

Bauman, Z. (1998) *Globalization: The Human Consequences*, Oxford: Polity Press.

Beck, U. (2001) *What is Globalisation?* Oxford: Polity Press.

Beck, U. (1992) *Risk Society: Towards a New Modernity*, London: Sage.

Bentley, T. (1998) *Learning Beyond the Classroom: Education for a Changing World*, London: Routledge/DEMOS.

Blackburn, S. (2001) *Being Good*, New York: Oxford University Press.

Blunkett, D. (1999) *Conference Speech*, Education in Human Rights Network 6th Annual Conference, Sheffield, June, 1999.

Broughton, S., Ellingham, M., Muddyman, D. and Trillo, R (eds). (1994) *World Music: The Rough Guide*, London: Penguin Books.

Bruner, J. (1996) *The Culture of Education*, Cambridge, MA: Harvard University Press.

Burns, S. and Lamont, G. (1995) *Values and Visions*, London: Hodder and Stoughton.

Castells, M. (1991) *The Informational City*, Oxford: Basil Blackwell.

Clough, N. (1999) Education for Citizenship: understanding the perspectives and practice of parents. Unpublished paper for BERA conference, 1999.

Clough, N. and Tarr J. (2000) 'The role of dance in cultural development', in M. Kear, and G. Callaway (eds). *Improving Teaching and Learning in the Arts,* London: Falmer.

Clough, N. (1998) 'Emerging from the tunnel: some dilemmas in environmental education', in C. Holden and N. Clough (eds) *Children as Citizens, Education for Participation.* London: Jessica Kingsley.

Council of Europe (1985) Recommendation No. R(85)7 of the Committee of Ministers, Appendix 3.2, Strasbourg: Council of Europe.

Crewe, I. (1996) 'Comparitive Research Findings', in QCA (1998) *Education for Citizenship and the Teaching of Democracy in Schools.* London: QCA/DfEE.

Crick, B. (1998) in *Times Educational Supplement* (TES) 4/09/98.

Crick, B. (2000) *Essays on Citizenship. London: Continuum.*

Davies, I. and Rey M. (1998) 'Questionning identities', in C. Holden and N. Clough (eds) *Children as Citizens, Education for Participation.* London: Jessica Kingsley.

Davies, L. (1998) *School Councils and Pupil Exclusions.* London: School Councils, UK.

Dewey, J. (1900) *The School and Society,* Chicago: University Press.

DfEE, (1998) *The National Literacy Strategy,* London: DfEE.

DfEE/QCA, (1999) *The National Curriculum,* London: DfEE/QCA.

Edwards, D. and Mercer, N. (1987) *Common Knowledge,* London: Methuen.

Elliott, J. (1998) *The Curriculum Experiment: Meeting the Challenge of Social Change,* Buckingham: OUP.

Epstein, D. (1993) *Changing Classroom Cultures: Anti-racism, Politics and Schools,* Stoke-on-Trent: Trentham.

Etzioni, A. (1997) *The New Golden Rule: Community and Morality in a Democratic Society*, New York: Basic Books.

Fennes, H. and Hapgood K. (1997) *Intercultural Learning in the Classroom: Crossing the Borders*, Council of Europe, London: Cassell.

Fawcett, M. and Duckett, R. (2000) *Brief Exhibition Guide, The Hundred Languages of Children*, Newcastle Upon Tyne: Sightlines Initiative.

Fisher, S. (1980) *Ideas into Action: Curriculum for a Changing World*, London: World Studies Project.

Fisher, S. and Hicks, D. (1985) *World Studies 8–13: A Teacher's Handbook*, Edinburgh: Oliver and Boyd.

Freire, P. (1972) *Education: The Pedagogy of the Oppressed*, Penguin: London.

Gilbert, R. (1995) 'Education for citizenship and the problem of identity in post-modern political culture', in J. Ahier and A. Ross (eds) *The Social Subjects within the Curriculum; Children's Social Learning in the National Curriculum*, London: Falmer.

Griffith, I. (1996) *Research Paper on the Peer Mediation Project*, Edinburgh: The Scottish Council for Research in Education.

Griffith, R. (1996) 'New powers for old: transforming power relationships', in M. John (ed.) *Children in Our Charge: The Child's Right to Resources*, London: Jessica Kingsley.

Grugeon, E. *et al.* (1998) *Teaching Speaking and Listening in the Primary School*, London: Fulton.

Gundara, J. (2000) *Interculturalism, Education and Inclusion*, London: Paul Chapman.

Harber, C. (1998) 'Education and democracy in Britain and Southern Africa', in C. Harber, C. (ed.) *Voices for Democracy*, Nottingham: Education Now.

Hargreaves, D.H. (1982) *The Challenge for the Comprehensive School: Culture, Curriculum and Community*, London: Routledge and Kegan Paul.

Harwood, D. (1984) 'The World Studies 8–13 Project and Political Education: some problems of dissemination', *Curriculum* 5: 30–36.

Hicks, D. and Holden C. (1995) *Visions of the Future: Why we Need to Teach for Tomorrow*, Stoke on Trent: Trentham.

Hicks, D. and Steiner, M. (eds) (1989) *Making Global Connections: A World Studies Workbook*, Stoke on Trent: Trentham.

Hoggett, P. (1997) *Enough is Enough: Contested Communities*, Southampton: Hobbs the Printers.

Holden, C. and Clough N. (1998) 'The teacher's role in assisting participation', in C. Holden and N. Clough (eds) *Children as Citizens: Education for Participation*, London: Jessica Kingsley.

Huckle, J. (1996) 'Globalisation, postmodernity and citizenship', in M. Steiner (ed.) *Developing the Global Teacher*, Stoke-on-Trent: Trentham.

Jowell, R. and Park, A. (1997) 'Young people, politics and citizenship: a disengaged generation?' in QCA (1998) *Education for Citizenship and the Teaching of Democracy in Schools*, London: QCA.

Katz, D. (2000) *People Funny Boy: the Genius of Lee 'Scratch' Perry*, Edinburgh: Payback Press.

Klein, G. in *Times Educational Supplement* (TES) 30/10/98.

Kushner, S. (1991) *The Children's Music Book: Performing Musicians in School*, London: Gulbenkian Foundation.

Makhudu, N. (1993) Cultivating a climate of Cupertino through Ubuntu. *Enterprise*, 68: 40–1.

Meisels, S.J., Atkins-Burnett, S. and Nicholson, J. (1995) 'Assessment of social competence, adaptive behaviours and approaches to learning with young children'. University of Michigan briefing paper for the National Center for Educational Statistics.

Midwinter, C. (1994) 'Watching the world: curriculum strategies for teaching about the media', in A. Osler (ed.) *Development Education: Global Perspectives in the Curriculum*, London: Cassell.

Osler, A. (1998) 'Conflicts, controversy and caring: young people's attitudes towards children's rights', in C. Holden and N. Clough (eds) *Children as Citizens, Education for Participation*, London: Jessica Kingsley.

Parekh, B. (2000) *Rethinking Multiculturalism: Cultural Diversity and Political Theory*, London: Macmillan Press.

Pike, G. and Selby, D. (1988) *Global Teacher, Global Learner*, London: Hodder and Stoughton.

Policy Studies Institute (1997) *Ethnic Minorities in Britain: Diversity and Disadvantage*, London: Policy Studies Institute.

Pollard, A. and Filer, A. (1996) *The Social World of Children's Learning*, London: Cassell.

Posch, P. and Mair, G. (1997) 'Dynamic networking and community collaboration: the cultural scope of education action research', in S. Hollingsworth (ed.) *International Action Research – A Casebook for Educational Reform*, London: Falmer.

QCA, (1998) *Education for Citizenship and the Teaching of Democracy in Schools*, London: QCA.

139

QCA, (2000) *PSHE and Citizenship at Key Stage 1 and 2. Initial Guidance for Schools*, London: QCA.

Richardson, R. (1976) *Learning for Change in World Society*, London: One World Trust.

Rogers, C. (1983) *Freedom to Learn for the Eighties*, Columbus, OH: Merrill.

Rowe, D. (1996) *The Business of School Councils: Draft Report*, London: The Citizenship Foundation.

Rudduck, J. (1995) *School Improvement: What Can Pupils Tell Us?* London: David Fulton.

Rudduck, J., Wallace, G. and Day, J. (1997) 'Student voices: what can they tell us as "partners in change"?' in K. Stott, and V.N. Trafford (eds) *Partners in Change: Shaping the Future*, London: Middlesex University.

Runnymede, (2000) *The Future of Multi-Ethnic Britain*, The Parekh Report, London: Profile Books.

Said, E. (1993) *Culture and Imperialism*, London: Chatto and Windus.

Sellman, E. (2000) 'Building bridges: preparing children for secondary school'. *Pastoral Care in Education*, 18: 27–9.

Short, C. (1999) *Education and our Future*, Annual Conference of the Secondary Heads Association, DFID.

Spurgeon, C. (1998) 'Citizenship education through literature', in C. Holden and N. Clough (ed.), *Children as Citizens: Education for Participation*, London: Jessica Kingsley.

Stacey, H. (1996) 'Mediation into schools does go! An outline of the mediation process and how it can be used to promote positive relationships and effective conflict resolution in schools' *Pastoral Care in Education* 14: 7–9.

Starkey, H. (1992) 'Back to Basic Values: education for justice and peace in the world', *Journal of Moral Education*, 21:185–92.

Stenhouse, L. (1980) 'Curriculum research and the art of the teacher', *Curriculum*, 1: 40–4.

Stevens, O. (1982) *Children Talking Politics*, Oxford: Martin Robinson Publishers.

Talbot, M. and Tate, N. (1997) 'Shared values in a pluralist society?' in R. Smith, and P. Standish (eds) *Teaching Right and Wrong: Moral Education in the Balance*, Stoke on Trent: Trentham.

Tanner, J. (1998) 'Speaking for ourselves, listening to others: young global citizens learning through the study of distant places', in C. Holden and N. Clough (eds), *Children as Citizens: Education for Participation*, London: Jessica Kingsley.

Trafford, B. (1993) *Sharing Power in Schools: Raising Standards*, Nottingham: Education Now.

Tyrrell, J. and Farrell, S. (1995) *Peer Mediation in Primary Schools*, Coleraine: University of Ulster.

Wilkinson, H. and Mulgan, G. (1995) 'Freedom's Children; work, relationships and politics for 18–34-year-olds in Britain today', in QCA (1998) *Education for Citizenship and the Teaching of Democracy in Schools*, London: QCA.

Wood, A. and Richardson, R. (1992) *Inside Stories; Wisdom and Hope for Changing Worlds*, Stoke-on-Trent: Trentham.

Wood, L. (1998) 'Participation and Learning in Early Childhood', in C. Holden and N. Clough, *Children as Citizens: Education for Participation*, London: Jessica Kingsley.

Further recommended reading

Alvarado, M. and Boyd-Barratt, O. (1992) *Media Education: An Introduction*. London: BFI with OU.

Buckingham, D. (2000) *The Making of Citizens: Young People, News and Politics*, London: Routledge.

Cogan, J. and Derricott, R. (2000) *Citizenship for the 21st Century: An International Perspective on Education*, London: Kegan Paul.

Claire, H. (2001) *Not Aliens: Primary School Children and the Citizenship/PSHE Curriculum*, Stoke-on-Trent: Trentham.

Grimwade, K. *et al.* (2000) *Geography and the New Agenda*, Sheffield: The Geographical Association.

Nichols, A. and Kinninment, D. (eds) (2001) *More Thinking Through Geography*, Cambridge: Chris Kington.

Osler, A. (ed.) (2000) *Citizenship and Democracy in Schools: Diversity, Identity, Equality*, Stoke-on-Trent: Trentham.

Osler, A. and Starkey, H. (1996) *Teacher Education and Human Rights*, London: Fulton.

Richardson, R. and Wood, A. (1999) *Inclusive Schools, Inclusive Society: Race and Identity on the Agenda*, Stoke-on-Trent: Trentham.

Silcock, P. and Stacey, H. (1996) 'Peer mediation and the cooperative school' *Education 3 to 13*, June 1997.

Walton, K. (1995) *Picture My World: Photography in the Primary Classroom*, London: ACGB.

Practical resources and training materials

Action Aid (1998) *City by the Sea: Urban Development in Mombasa, Kenya, (Key Stages 3 and 4).* Action Aid.

Amnesty International: *Just Right: an Educational CD-Rom and Teachers' Workbook.*

Burns, S. and Lamont, G. (1996) *Values and Visions: A Handbook for Spiritual Development and Global Awareness,* London: Hodder and Stoughton

Bliss, T. and Robinson, G. (1995) *Developing Circle Time.* Lucky Duck Publications.

Brown, M. (ed) (1996) *Our World, Our Rights: Teaching About Rights and Responsibilities in the Primary Classroom,* London: Amnesty International.

Brown, M. and Harrison, D. (1996) *Changing Childhoods: a Sourcebook for Teaching 8–12s about Children and Social Change in Britain since the 1930s,* London: SCF.

Clay, D. with Gold, J. (2000) *Primary School Councils Toolkit,* London: School Councils UK.

Christian Aid (2000) *Local Citizen: Global Citizen. Activities for Teaching Citizenship and Personal Development for Use with 8–12 year olds.* London: Christian Aid.

Combes, A. (2001) *21st Century Citizens.* (Teacher Pack and Pupil book), Cable Education.

Collins, J. (1994) *Maths Matters: Examples of Mathematics in the Environment* (Key Stages 3 and 4), WWF.

Davies, L. and Najda, R. (2001) *Wall to Wall Design* (activities for KS3 on sustainable housing around the world). ITDG Publishing or *www.oneworld.org/itdg*

Dawes, L., Mercer, N. and Wegerif, R. (2000) *Thinking Together: a programme of activities for developing thinking skills at KS2.* Questions Publications.

D.E.C. (Birmingham) (1999) *A Different Story: Writing to Open Up the World at Key Stage 2.* Birmingham: Development Education Centre.

D.E.C. (Birmingham) (1999) *Writing our Past: Celebrating and Researching the Achievements of People in the Past who Came to Live in Britain.* Birmingham: Development Education Centre.

DfID/Action Aid (2000) *Learning Global Lessons: 50 Non-Fiction Literacy Hours,* DfID/Action Aid.

European, Youth Centre (1995) *All Different, All Equal. Education Pack for Intercultural Education with Young People and Adults.* Copies available free (in English or French) from the Youth Directorate, 30 rue Pierre de Coubertin, F-67000 Strasbourg, France.

Fountain, S. (1995) *Education for Development: a Teacher's Resource Book for Global Development,* London: Hodder and Stoughton.

Hicks, D. (2001) *Citizenship for the Future: A Practical Classroom Guide,* Godalming: WWF-UK.

Grimwade, K. *et al.* (2000) *Geography and the New Agenda,* Sheffield: The Geographical Association.

Jarvis, H. and Midwinter, C. (1999) *Talking Rights; Taking Responsibility. A Speaking and Listening Resource for Secondary English and Citizenship.* UNICEF.

Mosley, J. (1996) *Quality Circle Time.* LDA.

*Oxfam (2001) *Your World, My World: A Wake Up World Photopack for Citizenship, PSE and PSD,* Oxfam.

Oxfam (1998) *Making a Meal of it: Photoset and Activities for 7–11 year olds, Looking at Food Issues Around the World,* Oxfam.

Oxfam (2000) *Photo Opportunities 2000: photos from around the world for the primary classroom.* Oxfam

Parliament: Fact Sheets on Elections, Government, Debates, Making Laws and the Houses of Commons and Lords, available from: Parliamentary Education Unit, Room 604, Norman Shaw Building, London SW1A 2TT

Pike, G. and Selby, D. (1995) *Reconnecting: From National to Global Curriculum,* WWF-UK.

Pike, G. and Selby, D. (1995) *Earthkind. A Teachers' Handbook on Humane Education,* Stoke-on-Trent: Trentham.

Rowe, D. (2001) *Introducing Citizenship* (Teachers handbook and video guide), A&C Black with the Citizenship Foundation.

Rowe, D. and Newton J. (eds) (1994) *You, Me, Us – A New Approach to Moral and Social Education for Primary Schools.* Citizenship Foundation.

Rutter, J. (1998) *Refugees: A Resource Book for Primary Schools.* The Refugee Council.

Steele, P. (2001) *Citizenship,* Evans Publishing Group.

Steiner M. (1993) *Learning from Experience: A World Studies Source Book,* Stoke-on-Trent: Trentham.

SCF (1999) *The School Council: A Children's Guide.* SCF.

*SCF (1999) *Families Photopack.* Save the Children (SCF).

SCF (2000) *Partners in Rights – Creative Activities Exploring Rights and Citizenship for 7–11 year olds.* SCF.

Thinking Series (The Sand Tray, William and the Guinea Pig, Joe's Car, The Scary Video) (2001) A&C Black.

The Chocolate Trade Papapaa. A resource for Key Stage 2 for teaching about chocolate and fair trade. Available free from Educational Communications, The Tower Building, 11 York Road, London SE1 7NX. Tel 020 7401 4000.

UNICEF: *Know, Your Rights: Children's Rights in Plain English.*

Wright, P. (ed) (1999) *The Maths and Human Rights Resource Book: Bringing Human Rights into the Secondary Mathematics Classroom,* London: Amnesty International.

Young, M. with Commins, F. (2002) *Global Citizenship: The handbook for primary teaching,* Oxfam.

*particularly suitable for 'Most likely to ...' in Chapter 7.

Videos

Caring for our School and Friends: a School Council Experience. Schools Council U.K.

Exploring Beyond the Brochure: Issues for the Gambia, Issues for you. (Video and teachers' booklet). Tourism Concern.

Across and Beyond: Citizenship for Primary Schools. (Video and teachers' book). (2000) BBC.

Our News, Our Views: Children's Rights, Labour and the Media. (Video and teachers' activity pack for upper secondary) Anti-Slavery International.

Student text books (secondary)

Citizenship in Focus series (J. Foster ed.) Collins Educational:
Democracy in action
The citizen and the law
Human rights
Teachers' resource book
Oxfam series for 11–16 year olds:
Making peace
Developing rights
Dealing with disasters
Citizenship Foundation series (T. Thorpe ed.) Hodder and Stoughton
Understanding citizenship 1, 2, 3.

Contacts

Action Aid has educational resources and services for schools relating to citizenship: Chataway House, Leach Rd, Chard TA20, 1FR. www.actionaid.org.

Amnesty International, has many resources for both primary and secondary. Amnesty International, 1 Easton Street, London WC1X, 0DJ. www.amnesty.org.

Anti-Slavery International: Thomas Clarkson House, Bromsgrove Road, London SW9 9TL. www.antislavery.org.

Christian Aid has materials for teachers on R.E., literacy, geography and citizenship and staff who will visit schools. *www.christian-aid.org.uk.*

Citizenship Foundation provides case studies and competitions for students: 15 St Swithin's Lane, London EC4N 8AL (020 7929 3344) *www.citfou.org.uk.*

Centre for Citizenship Studies in Education: School of Education, University of Leicester, Leicester, LE1 7RF. *www.le.ac.uk/education/centres/citizenship* .

Centre for Thinking Skills: Brunel University College, 300 St Margaret's Road, Twickenham, TW1 1PT. (020 8891 0121).

The Children's Society helps schools design projects for the community: Margery Street, London WC1X 0JL *www.the-children-society.org.uk.*

Community links is a national network of local contacts. It produces an annual of innovative ideas, many by young people, which can be adapted for school. Community Links, 105 Baring Road, London, E16 4HQ (020 7473 2270).

Development Education Association (DEA): National umbrella for local centres providing materials and support for global education. DEA, 29–31 Cowper St., London EC2 4AT. *www.dea.org.uk* .

Hansard Society aims to educate about parliament and government, provides materials for schools to run mock elections: St Philips Building, LSE, Sheffield St, London, WC2 2EX. *www.hansardsociety.org.uk.*

Heartstone works with primary and secondary pupils to challenge racism and intolerance through story (real and fictional): Heartstone, Mayfield, Dingwall, Scotland, IV 15 9SS. Email: *sitakumari@heartstone.co.uk.*

Institute for Citizenship provides resources and training: 62 Marylebone High St, London W1M 3AF. *www.citizen.org.uk* .

Letterbox Library has a wide range of books with bi-lingual texts and excellent books celebrating equality and diversity. (020 7503 4801) *info@letterboxlibrary.com.*

Peer mediation training: Mediation U.K., Alexander House, Telephone Avenue, Bristol, BS1 4BS (0117 904 6661) E-mail: *mediationuk@cix.compulink.co.uk.*

Save the Children (SCF) has many materials for teachers and children: 17 Grove Lane, London SE5 8RD. *www.savethechildren.org.uk.*

Schools Council UK, 57 Etchingham Park Road, Finchley, London, N3 2EB.

Sustrans Safe Routes to Schools: provides free project material for schools to help make cycling and walking safer. *www.sustrans.org.uk.*

UNICEF provides information, resources and links with children around the world: 55 Lincoln's Inn Fields, London WC2A 3NB *www.unicef.org.uk.*

WWF-UK (World Wide Fund for Nature) has many resources for schools: Panda House, Weyside Park, Godalming, Surrey GU7 1XR. *www.wwf-uk.org.*

Websites

ecs.lewisham.gov.uk/citizens has examples of good practice in ICT/citizenship relating to the work of local councils. Lesson plans and activities for primary and secondary.

www.annefrank.eril.net/teaching/citizen.htm for material on Anne Frank and cross curricular issues.

www.article12.uk.com/ is a website run by young people for young people, showing them doing things for themselves.

www.britkid.org has been written for young people who do not live in ethnically diverse areas: it's informative, fun and very accessible.

www.citizen21.org.uk for materials, information and other links about democracy and rights issues. Free schools pack. Instigated by Charter 88.

www.comicrelief.com/education has a variety of lesson plans on topical issues and a children's interactive site.

www.dfes.gov.uk/citizenship for news, resources, other website links related to citizenship.

www.earthtimes.org for good background information for teachers.

www.eco-schools.org.uk for free materials to enable schools to carry out an environmental review and make an action plan.

www.education.ed.ac.uk/efs for active learning in environmental education.

www.electoral-reform.org.uk has information on the different electoral systems.

www.environment-agency.gov.uk for environmental issues at secondary level.

143

www.explore.parliament.uk for teachers' resources and activities for students (both primary and secondary) on all aspects of parliament.

www.foodandfarming.org.uk for activities for secondary schools on geography and sustainability issues.

www.gksoft.com/govt/en/ for access to other countries' governmental sites to help compare their constitution with the British system.

www.globalfootprints.org for activities for primary children related to sustainability.

www.globalgang.org.uk for termly newspaper for 8–12 year olds and website with teachers' section.

www.gn.apc.org/tourismconcern for information on sustainability and tourism.

www.homebeats.co.uk for resources on tackling racism.

www.learn.co.uk for activities and teaching materials on topical issues.

www.number-10.gov.uk/default.asp?pageid=8 is a young person's guide to Downing Street and British politics. Students can put questions to a minister and decide what they would do if they were prime minister.

www.oxfam.org.uk/coolplanet/ is aimed at children 6–16, is interactive and has many resources and links to useful sites.

www.standards.dfes.gov.uk/schemes for QCA schemes of work for secondary citizenship.

www.think-energy.com for curriculum resources on energy use.

www.wastewatch.org.uk for environmental issues at primary level.

www.wwflearning.co.uk for case studies relating to sustainability and environmental issues.

Index